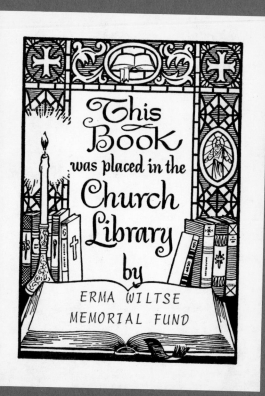

# A MEDITATOR'S DIARY

# A MEDITATOR'S DIARY

### A Western Woman's Unique
### Experiences in Thailand Temples

## Jane Hamilton-Merritt

*1817*

## HARPER & ROW, PUBLISHERS

New York, Hagerstown, San Francisco, London

FIRST U.S.EDITION

ISBN: 0-06-065563-1

LIBRARY OF CONGRESS CATALOG CARD NUMBER: 76-10001

76 77 78 79 80 10 9 8 7 6 5 4 3 2 1

*Gratefully, I dedicate this book*

to *Josie Stanton* for your loving-kindness and valuable insights into Buddhism

**and**

to *Harrison E. Salisbury* for encouraging me to publish this work.

## SPECIAL THANKS

To Khunying Arun Kitiyakara and Khun Thawin Pongsamart for your concerned assistance in helping me in my search for an understanding of your way of life.

To the Buddhist communities of Wat Bovornives, Wat Sraket, and Wat Muang Mang – especially to the patient and kind teaching monks.

Also to my friends, Elizabeth Sewell, William Bradley, Konrad Bekker and Sarah Bekker for your contributions in making this book a reality.

And to 'Buzz' for your inspiring and loving support of my intellectual pursuits.

# CONTENTS

# FOREWORD
by Harrison E. Salisbury

THERE is in the West today a growing sense of alienation, of the failure of Western philosophy, Western psychology and Western religion to cope with the ever-more complex problems which the post-industrial age has brought to mankind.

The earlier conviction of certainty, of absolute faith, of the superiority of Western logic and Western thinking to resolve any challenges which Man might encounter, has gradually been eroded by the increasing failure of science to meet human needs.

The iron positivism of a Cromwell, the sublime certainty of the 18-century Church of Rome and 19-century Protestantism, have vanished, and once again Man is left to struggle with the ever-widening gap between his perception of reality and the instruments which he can employ to help him comprehend that reality and his place within it.

No longer can there be doubt that the spreading sense of the futility and inadequacy of Western concepts underlies the explosion of interest in Eastern religion and philosophy which is now sweeping the West.

Of course, it is true that this explosion has long been in the building. Even before World War I active exploration of Eastern knowledge and culture was well advanced – particularly the knowledge and culture of India. So far as China was concerned there was scholarly (but hardly popular) interest in Confucianism. Japan was virtually untouched. So was Southeast Asia, although the mysteries of Tibet and Mongolia had long attracted the curious and the esoteric.

However, it is fair to say that popular interest in Buddhism, and specifically in its central concept of meditation, is of extremely recent origin, almost entirely a post-World War II phenomenon. This is especially true for Americans whose attention first began to be directed toward Zen Buddhism, for example, only during the 1960s, coincident with the sudden appearance of the hippie movement.

Interest in meditation, once stimulated, seems to have grown with remarkable speed in all Western countries. There are doubtless many reasons for this but the overriding one, or so it would seem to me, is the widening gap between Man and his technological milieu. The typical habitant of Technologia is highly educated, highly motivated, anti-religious or a-religious in the formal sense, sophisticated, urban and very often Freudian or Jungian. And the resident of Technologia, she or he, very often is unable to 'put it all together'. Life seems to possess no meaning. Existence contains neither ease nor satisfaction. The very act of existence seems insolently oppressive. Who am I (the identity crisis)? Where are we going (concern over civilization's ability to survive)? Why (the meaning of existence)? These are the questions heard again and again in New York, London, Paris, Moscow, Rome and Los Angeles. There are no answers.

It is the existence of this phantasmagoria of disconnection and disassociation which has directed so many to the East in search of an answer. Gurus become a Pop phenomenon. Zen comes to Broadway and Piccadilly. Dick Cavett brings Transcendental Meditation to national television, and suddenly the initials TM becomes as familiar as ABC.

In the huffing, puffing and hullabaloo no one notices that behind the talk and the television there is little content. Who actually knows or understands meditation as it is taught in the Buddhist East?

This, perhaps, is the central question, and it is that admirable service which Jane Hamilton-Merritt renders – she knows. She knows because she has had the endurance (and it does take endurance), the imagination (which so few possess), and the sympathetic understanding (the key to it all) to learn. To learn not merely from studying the Buddhist texts and the teachings of the Masters, but by *personal experience*. Alone, or almost alone among Westerners, she has gone to a teaching wat in northern Thailand, has sat at the feet of a genuine master, has lived the lonely, harsh and dangerous life of an acolyte in the cell. She has returned to describe her experience in tones so delicate, terms so precise and with such a bubbling sense of personal involvement that we find ourselves racing through her pages and ultimately, like Jane Hamilton-Merritt, actually capturing a sense of meditating.

We learn that meditation is not easy. It should not be undertaken lightly. It probably is not the thing for all, although all could benefit from it. It takes patience and fortitude. You do not simply sit in the half-lotus position, fix your eyes on a distant spot and begin to meditate. It is hard and it must be learned and practised.

But its rewards are great. Not easily described but palpable and tangible. It can bring the meditator understanding, deep insight, and relaxation, a new awareness of self, a revelation of depths in psyche and in the world such as cannot be imagined.

Meditation is central to Buddhism. It brings richness to life unlike that of any other human process. It may not afford the only avenue by which Man and Technologia can become reconciled, but it possesses potentials no other technique can match. Meditation may be the only thing which will make the post-industrial world habitable. Jane Hamilton-Merritt's experience will suggest to almost everyone why this can be true.

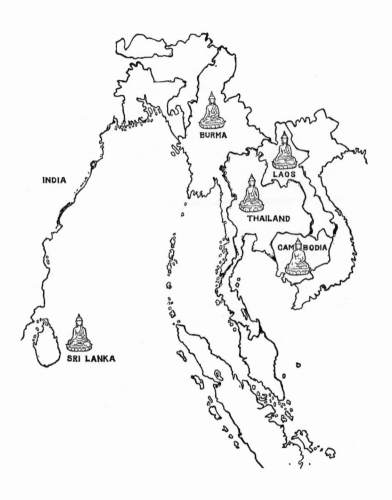

INDIA

BURMA

LAOS

THAILAND

CAMBODIA

SRI LANKA

# INTRODUCTION

THE road from the cornfields of Indiana where I grew up to the Buddhist temples of Southeast Asia has been long, arduous, frustrating, and often painful. This road, stretching half way around the world, carried me to Japan to attend graduate school; to Cambodia, Burma, Thailand and Laos to live among their peoples; to South Vietnam's southern deltas, to its Demilitarized Zone at the 17th parallel to photograph and write about the war and all the peoples involved; to remote mountainous villages inhabited by opium-growing ethnic minorities with whom I lived and about whom I wrote; and eventually into Buddhist temples where I became a part of the religious community and learned of Theravada Buddhism and meditation.

The inspiration for this long journey, which spanned over a decade, began when I, as a child of ten, encountered Pearl Buck's books on China. I knew that one day, I, too, would travel to those lands to see the peoples and cultures for myself. When I grew up, Americans were forbidden to travel to China, but politics did not diminish my desire to know more about Asian peoples and their cultures. Little did I know that one day I would be sitting before a Buddhist monk in a small temple in Northern Thailand struggling to learn Buddhist meditation.

As I learned more and more about the Southeast Asian cultures, particularly those of Burma, Cambodia, Laos, and Thailand, I came to realize that the role of Buddhism in their lives and psyche was paramount to the understanding of these peoples. I became more and more interested in this Southeast Asian form of Buddhism known as Theravada Buddhism and tried to involve myself in it. But this was difficult. I could go to the temples, or 'wats' and observe, which I often did. I could attend ceremonies with my Asian friends and I could talk with religious people, but I never became a part of the community.

I was never on the inside; I remained the 'farang', the foreigner.

In Thailand the temple buildings, sun-drenched in yellows, whites, and saffrons a-twinkle with blue and green mosaic glasswork, number almost twenty-four thousand. Some wats are grand edifices maintained by royalty; most are simple. No matter how humble they are elegant in design. The temples supported by the general population of forty million are the expressed devotion of a people to their religion. The village temple is the centre of the traditional Thai community; it functions as an inn for travellers, a seat of learning, a location for festivals, a playground for children, a haven for solace and spiritual comfort, as well as a refuge for those who become monks.

Unlike the Catholic priesthood, one does not become a Buddhist monk for life. One can enter and leave the monastery almost at will providing he has not committed a crime, nor is in debt, nor is using the monkhood as an escape from an undesirable social situation. Because of the flexibility in entering and leaving the monkhood, it is difficult to ascertain the exact number of monks, 'bhikku', in the Thai wats at any one time. It is estimated that annually one hundred and fifty thousand men are full-fledged monks, ninety thousand young men under twenty years of age are novices, and another one hundred and twenty thousand younger boys, called 'dek wat' (children of the wat) live in the temples as helpers.

Most Thai men intend to become a monk sometime in their young adult lives. One must be twenty-one before he can become a monk. Some men stay in the wat for only a few days, others for the three months of 'Khaow Pansa', the 'Rains Retreat' period, others stay for years and a few for a lifetime. There is no pressure to stay or leave; it is the individual's decision entirely. Not all Thai men enter the monkhood in their twenties, some enter after their families are raised and their responsibilities are lessened. I observed the ordination of a Thai man in Bangkok whose grandson gave him his alms bowl and saffron robes during the ceremony. To become a monk, to study the teachings of Buddha, and to live the ascetic, though not harsh, life is the best way to make merit. The making of merit helps give one the spiritual capability that will enable the Buddhist to pursue the ultimate goal of 'nirvana', the cessation of rebirth. Since women cannot become monks, one of the most important ways for women to gather merit is through their sons when they join the community of monks, the 'Sangha'.

A few words about the Thai people, their origins and their history seems essential. First it is important to understand that the definitive history of Thailand is unknown. Almost yearly new scholarly research brings new data to our knowledge of that area. Only recently archeologists digging in Northeast Thailand found pottery that startled experts. This controversial pottery, known as Ban Chiang after one of the villages in which it was found, is believed by some experts to have been made as early as 4,500 BC – that's almost 7,000 years ago! Whose hands made these ancient pots? Scholars don't yet know. But the reddish designs of twirling spirals lure us to speculate on their aged origins. So archeologists continue to dig and historians continue to struggle to piece together a history of Thailand.

Amidst all this ambiguity, it is known that some T'ai peoples, which include the Shan, Lao, and Thai, originally inhabited an area in eastern China south of the Yangtze River. Later, they moved into the plateaus of the great mountain ranges in China's present-day Yunnan Province. Along these mountainous river valleys some Thai and other ethnic minorities moved southward in large groups during the 13th century when Kublai Khan swept over Southern China. Over the centuries, the T'ai peoples continued a migrational flow southward to escape the encroachment of Chinese population movements and consequent demands for land. To this day, even lesser minority groups, now referred to as hilltribe people, move along the same migrational routes that some of the Thai probably travelled to look for land and a better life.

These Thai refugees brought with them from their high-plateaued home a pervasive belief in ancestor worship and animism. Their animistic beliefs held that elements of nature, such as trees, rocks, rivers, mountains had spirits which had to be propitiated and worshipped. In their new homelands in the Mekong and Chao Phraya river valleys, the Thai encountered the Hindu-inspired gods and demons of the Khmer civilization whose influence reached far from the capital of Angkor. They also encountered Theravada Buddhism through the Mon peoples, the indigenous inhabitants of the area who were conquered by the Khmers. The Mon peoples, whose ancient capitals originally were in Southern Burma and Thailand, have preserved their language and culture only in small areas in these countries. Both the Khmer and Mon civilizations were moulded by Indian cultural influences, especially Hinduism and Buddhism.

Although the origins of some of the Thai people can be traced to present day China, the Thai do not think of their heritage as Chinese. It was from the Chinese that some groups of Thai had fled their ancestral homeland. Culturally the Thais were influenced to a greater extent by the Indian culture than the Chinese. The Thai language is a tonal, monosyllabic language laced with Pali and Sanskrit words. With five tones, an alphabet comprising 44 consonants and 24 vowels, and a script reminiscent of Pali and Sanskrit, the Thai language can present real problems for Western students.

There is confusion in Western circles about the differences between Theravada and Mahayana sects of Buddhism. The Theravadists chose to adhere to what they term the orthodox school which follows more closely the Buddha's original teachings. This group stresses the role of the individual in seeking his own liberation, or 'nirvana', with the Buddha as teacher not a god. The Mahayanists follow a more liberal interpretation than the Theravada school. This group introduced the deification of the Buddha and the concept of Bodhisattvas, enlightened beings who chose to remain among men to teach them the way of salvation, which diminished the importance of the concept that nirvana could only be obtained by individual effort. In the West, Theravada Buddhism is often referred to as Hinayana, or the Lesser Vehicle. Theravada – meaning 'The Way of the Elders' – Buddhists consider Hinayana a pejorative term, one given to them by the liberal Mahayanists. Mahayana Buddhism found followers and flourished in Tibet, China, Japan, Korea, Sikkim and Vietnam.

In accepting the more orthodox ways, the Theravada Buddhists also chose to use the traditional Pali scriptures as opposed to those written in Sanskrit; thus, we find that the Theravadists employ the terms 'nibbana', 'dhamma', and 'kamma', which are the Pali forms. Pali was the language spoken by the Buddha. The Mahayanists use 'nirvana', 'dharma', and 'karma', the Sanskrit forms of the words. In the following chapters, I will employ the Pali forms since those are the ones employed by the Theravada Buddhists.

It seems that to embrace Theravada Buddhism the Thai people found it unnecessary to renounce their existing animistic and superstitious beliefs. Instead of casting off traditional beliefs, they added the new Buddhist concepts to the already existing plethora of ethereal creatures both malevolent and benevolent that roam the lands, often harassing and tempting people. Some of these creatures are called 'phii', or ghosts, who demand placation and the Thais acquiesce. Every home, apartment building and even hotel has a spirit house which is considered the abode of Chao Tii, a spirit of special rank. Chao Tii is the guardian spirit of the home or the hotel. Offerings to Chao Tii of food, incense, flowers, and candles are placed on the small platform surrounding the spirit house.

While twentieth century technology has permeated Thai daily life, particularly in Bangkok, in the forms of movies, radios, cars, television, Western dress, for the majority of Thai people the old traditions and beliefs remain unchanged by the superficial gadgets of the West.

The concept of the divinity of kings or the god-king cult was introduced into Thai culture during Cambodia's suzerainty over present-day Thailand and Laos. This concept was Brahmin in origin, but over the years it was tempered and modified by the Thai-Buddhist idea that a person of noble rank was born into nobility because of his karma. Thus, it was believed that

19

a king deserved to be king because of his previous meritorious lives. This resulted in the king not only being infallible, but a sacred being – a very highly evolved individual – who was revered by those still struggling with good and bad karma, hoping that in a coming life their good karma would elevate them to a higher state of respect.

Three years ago, I made the decision that my compelling interest in studying and possibly then writing about Buddhism should be taken seriously. I wanted to write about Theravada Buddhism as practised among the Southeast Asians, yet, in truth, I knew that I actually possessed no depth of understanding of Buddhism. I turned to philosophical treatises, most of them written by Westerners, but these writings only seemed to confuse my understanding. From my own observations, there seemed to be dimensions about the actual practice of Buddhism that differed considerably from the theories as expounded by Westerners. As I pursued this quest of trying to understand Theravada Buddhism, I eventually realized meditation to be a paramount dimension. I was puzzled and never quite able to understand what it was all about. I had friends who were students of Transcendental Meditation in the States and I was aware that meditation of the Theravada Buddhists was much deeper – a profound enlightening experience. In fact, it seemed to be a cultural experience.

In time, I decided that I would try to join a religious community. I soon found, however that I would encounter tremendous difficulties in finding a Buddhist monastery that would accept me – the foreign woman – as a resident. I tried for over a year with no success. My inquiries and requests to live within a wat compound were met with kind but negative responses. Usually I was told by the head monk that I could come to visit the wat any time, but as to the question of living in, the response was commonly that there were no facilities for women. I temporarily gave up my quest and returned to my home in Connecticut.

Finally, I learned of a wat in Bangkok that would teach meditation to foreigners on a day-student approach. Excited by the idea that I might be able to join a religious community even if it were on a very limited basis, I decided that I should go there and ask to be accepted as a student.

As I prepared for this journey into another world, I realized that my ignorance about Buddhism was enormous. My only advantages, it seemed, were my knowledge of the customs of the land, my adequate command of the Thai language, and my at-home feeling with the Thai people. On the other hand, I knew nothing about living in a wat or practising meditation. In fact, I had only known a few people who had practised Theravada meditation and were willing to talk about it. Some of their experiences had been successful; others not.

None of these acquaintances had ever told me what actually happens in meditation. They had only discussed it in general terms such as how meditation can be a peaceful experience, or how through the experience one can learn to be tranquil or gain a better understanding of one's self. All this sounded fine and, of course, I wanted to experience these things too, but how did it all come about?

Unfortunately, or perhaps most fortunately, I had never encountered a written description of anyone's experiences. I had read of Zen meditation but found no *experiential* writings on classical Theravada Buddhist meditation. I have recently discovered that some such books do exist, many printed by Buddhist societies in Southeast Asia, which could have been helpful in preparing me for my meditation journey. But on the other hand, I went into the experiences almost as a blank paper, not knowing, but desirous of knowing. With hindsight I suppose that in many ways this was a benefit, for I was not hampered with preconceived ideas nor did I have the opportunity to set up goals based on someone else's experiences.

I believe that the reason that there are so few meaningful experiential books on meditation is that the world of meditation almost defies written description since it takes one into worlds beyond . . . worlds without time, space, or form. And how does one, using the English language, describe a world for which this language is inadequate? I have found that trying accurately to describe the world of meditation has been my most difficult writing assignment.

As I packed to leave the States, my husband, whom I had married two years earlier in Bangkok, and I tried to focus on what it was that I was about to encounter. But even together, neither of us could have imagined the experiences that I would have. He was as excited as I was about my up-coming adventure, but he, not being a participant, did not feel the apprehensions that I harboured. His enthusiasm and interest in my pursuit gave me confidence that I would find my adventure a worthwhile endeavour. Little did we know that I was about to set out on what may be the most extraordinary experiences of my life.

I want to emphasize that this book is about Theravada Buddhist beliefs and practices. This form of Buddhism is not the Zen of Japan, nor the varieties of Buddhism known in China and Tibet. Neither is this book concerned with such Oriental practices as yoga or Transcendental Meditation. While Theravada Buddhism is quite special, there are many under-lying similarities among all forms of Buddhism, and one of the main common features is meditation, which reinforces experientially the tenets of the philosophy. It seems that each form of Buddhism reflects the distinct culture of the country in which it is practised, to the extent that histories, indigenous beliefs, and local customs freely co-mingle, forming a religious belief that, in essence, is a way of life. It seems to be true that in most Buddhist sects, meditation is the soul of the Buddhist experience.

Upon a cursory examination based on personal experience, it seems that the two types of meditation 'samadhi', tranquil-lity meditation and 'vipassana', insight meditation, that I en-countered in Thailand (and for that matter other meditation techniques) in their initial stages can both lead an individual to a finer development of the mind. It seems that these disci-plines can develop one's mind to become more centred and more still and, as a result, better able to understand a world that often seems confusing, unjust, painful and in constant flux.

Man – at least some men – has always sought to expand his mind, to search the unknown. Sometimes the result is a fanciful flight of poetry or a scientific journey into spaces beyond. Recent Western man has been experimenting with mind-expanding drugs that have produced not only interesting phenomena, but in some cases revolutionary thinking about the treatment of mental illness and the innate nature of man. At the same time, there have been rampant abuses and misuses of these drugs, and some tragic events. Meditation is a mind-expanding device, but a non-chemical one. In meditation one can stretch beyond known limits to allow the mind, with its seemingly endless dimensions, to explore, to discover, to go beyond what we traditionally have considered man's reality and not be subjected to abuses or possible devastating after-effects that drugs can cause.

In Theravada meditation, the mind is developed not to 'take a trip', nor to perform miracles, nor to foresee the future, nor to foretell winning lottery numbers (the latter three are forbidden by the Theravada Buddhist monastic code of right conduct). The desired goal of this meditation is, in general terms, to provide man with an opportunity to see the truth – that life is suffering; that all things are impermanent; and that the self is not personal, nor permanent, nor static; and, consequently that the individual does not exist as a permanent and identifiable entity. If man, according to the Theravada Buddhists, can come to know these truths, then, because of his understanding of these truths, he will be able to conduct himself in such a manner that sufferings will be lessened.

In my early days of meditation study I would sit in the coolness and shade of the courtyard of Wat Bovornives and think of the Buddha and the history of Buddhism. He was an Indian Prince – Siddartha Gautama by name – who became enlightened and consequently was called Buddha – the awakened or enlightened one. Born in present-day Nepal in the 6th century BC, this man eventually called Buddha lived to an old age – some say 80. He spent many years – maybe 45 – after his enlightenment as a wandering monk teaching the wisdom gained in his enlightenment. He referred to this general body of knowledge as the Middle Way. As a young man seeking to find solutions to the uneasiness and stress that is shared by all humans, Prince Siddartha tried extreme ascetecism until, it is said, he was near death. He concluded that mortification of the body did not bring knowledge and that extremes of any kind only cause unhappiness – thus, he called his path the Middle Way.

It is said that soon after his enlightenment, which took place under a bo tree at Buddha Gaya in India, he explained publicly his new-found knowledge. This knowledge was based on four concepts which became known as the 'four noble truths'. 1) that unhappiness exists 2) that there is a cause for that unhappiness 3) that unhappiness can cease 4) that there is a way that can lead to the cessation of unhappiness.

In those initial days of my study, I was truly mystified, wondering how these 'four truths' and the direction or path suggested by the last truth could be understood by me – particularly through the experience of meditation.

While I could only speculate on how I might, if ever, come to understand these teachings of Buddha, history was more definite. History records that Buddhism first flourished in India and Nepal. It eventually lost favour there, but over the years spread to much of the then known world – to Burma, Cambodia, Laos, Sri Lanka, Thailand, Vietnam, Tibet, Sikkim, China, Korea, Japan, Afghanistan, Siberia, and even into Eastern Europe.

In the midst of all my mental confusion, there was one note of hope for me. The Buddha did not demand from his followers a blind faith in his teachings. Instead, he taught that everyone must explore these teachings for him or her self so that the individual might come personally to see and to know the truth. This freedom of inquiry into the 'dhamma', his teachings, is still encouraged among Theravada Buddhists and this thought gave me courage to continue my struggle to understand. How different is this Buddhist idea from those religions that decree that faith alone will bring understanding!

The reflections and meditation episodes which follow are a compilation and condensation of experiences – both grand and small, but all meaningful – that happened to me, the novice.

If it seems that form, direction, or progress is lacking, it is because the nature of the experience often appeared outside traditional frames of reference and often outside common parameters of time and place as understood in Western terms.

This book is also about the experiences of one woman living in a Buddhist environment; of the fears, joys, doubts, pains and exaltations encountered in her first intensive meditation experience, and of the resultant meaning that this discipline has had in her life back in her home country. At the same time, I'm convinced that these meditation experiences and subsequent insights are not unique to just one individual but are common to all – Asian and non-Asian – who have practised intensive meditation.

My journey into Buddhism and meditation began at Wat Bovornives, a royal wat in Bangkok, Thailand. It is of this journey into a world beyond that I write.

# Chapter One

Meditation is the heart of the Buddhist Way . . .
                          Winston King, *One Thousand Lives*


VERY afraid, I approached the Abbot's 'guti'. As I kicked off
my sandals at the door of his little house, I could see a monk,
the Abbot, sitting Buddha-like in a mound of saffron robes
inside on the floor. A flurry of thoughts hurried through my
mind. 'Be sure to prostrate three times. Don't touch him.
Always keep the hands in a respectful "wai" position.'

As I waited in the doorway for him to acknowledge my
presence, I wanted to disappear. What was I doing here?
This was a man's world. Foreign women had no place in a
Buddhist wat. The red and saffron asters which I had brought
seemed heavy in my hands. 'He's important; he's the Abbot of
one of the royal wats of Thailand. Kings were ordained here,
including the present one. This is one of the most significant
wats in Bangkok. Do I dare enter this world?'

Finally he looked toward me. Awkwardly, flowers in my
hands, I approached him on my knees. 'Never let my head
be higher than his', I told myself again and again. When I had
crawled close to him, I laid the flowers aside and prostrated
three times, touching my head to the floor with my hands
held in prayer-like fashion. This was new and troublesome
because I did not know how to do it properly. Each time I
raised my head, I noticed that he was watching me, making
me even more nervous.

After the prostration, I sat on my knees, immobile, waiting.
He seemed to be staring through me. I felt that he could read
my mind. Unable to bear the silence, I, with my hands in a
wai before my face, tried to introduce myself and make my
request to study Buddhist meditation with him. He seemed
not to hear. He continued to stare at and through me. I
wondered what I had done wrong. I was wearing a high-
necked, long-sleeved, full-length dress which I had been told
was appropriate. Maybe I should not have spoken first? Sweat

trickled down my body from fear and heat, but mostly from fear.

He didn't answer, so I gathered up the flowers and extended them to him. Since neither he nor any monk can receive anything directly from a woman, he took a piece of saffron cloth and put it before me. I laid the flowers on the cloth and he pulled the cloth and flowers near him, but he didn't look at them nor say thank you to me.

I sat still, keeping my hands in the respectful wai position. I noticed that the right side of his mouth was twitching. Eventually he spoke, very softly and slowly in English. 'What do you know about Buddhism?'

I answered in a voice that was undoubtedly too loud and which expressed my fear. 'I've read books on Buddhism, but I've come here to study meditation.'

More empty minutes. He spoke again. 'What is meditation?'

Trying to hold my trembling voice to a softness resembling his, I answered. 'I don't really know. I've only read generally about it, but for me it seems impossible to know or to understand meditation by merely reading about it. That's why I want to study with you here at Wat Bovornives.'

It seemed as if he were looking inside me. What was he searching for? Sincerity? I did not know. But I knew that I was nervous, uncomfortable, and aware that I was out of the world which I knew. After some empty minutes he spoke. 'Dhamma class and meditation class meet tonight here in my guti at 6:00. You may come'.

I prostrated myself three times and backed out of the room on my knees. Outside I could barely stand. I fumbled with my sandals and with heavy heart walked slowly within the wat compound along a small 'klong' bridged with walk-overs. At one bridge, I sat down to reflect.

The late afternoon heat hung heavy in the air. Barefooted monks, robed in saffron with newly shaven heads, strolled by slowly. Sunspots edging through heavily leafed trees dabbled geometric designs on their robes. Erect, stately, like statues, they moved. An occasional breeze stirred their flowing robes. As I watched I became calm.

27

Why had I been so afraid? Thailand was not a new place for me. I was familiar with Thai ways. I had visited many wats and often found them a retreat from heat and noise. Wats had always been a place of contemplation for me. But this was different; I was trying to enter a way of life that demanded seclusion and meditation and was primarily open to men. Monks are not only celibate, but they must not touch a woman. They may speak to a woman, but only if another person is present. So it is easier not to have women living in wat compounds, particularly farang women.

I did not want to do something stupid or break a rule which would cause a monk to go through a complicated purification ceremony. But was I being overly sensitive?

As I waited for the evening class on dhamma, the teachings of Buddha, dusk descended into the compound. An evening breeze brushed the temple bells, which hung from the roof gables, producing a symphony of fragile tinkles. Delicate and yet omnipresent, the sound of the temple chimes brought back the serenity that I had always experienced on visits to wats.

It was here, in this particular wat, in the early 1800s, that Prince Mongkut spent fourteen years as the Abbot before becoming the King of Siam. It was here that this Prince, who was a philosopher, scientist, linguist and scholar, attempted to purify Buddhist philosophy by going back to the ancient Pali scriptures, to the original teachings of Buddha. As a result of his scholarly research, he found the strict Dhammayut sect in order to strengthen the rules of Theravada Buddhism which, in turn, greatly influenced the already existing sect known as Mahanikai.

As I reflected about the life of King Mongkut, perhaps one of the best minds among Oriental leaders in his time, I felt a sadness and a bit of rage because the West only knew this small man, who spent a total of twenty-six years in the monkhood, as a raucous degenerate, sometime tyrant, and often as a buffoon. All of this was dreamed up by one Anna Leonowens in her books, *The English Governess at the Siamese Court* and *The Romance of the Harem* which eventually became popularized by Yul Brunner in the play and then the movie, 'Anna and the King of Siam'. What a pity!

Here in this wat, a-tingle with the music of miniature bells, I soon forgot the contemptuous manner in which Americans thought of King Mongkut, to think of other famous people who had entered this wat to study the teachings of Buddha and to practice meditation. It was here that the present King of Thailand, Bhumipol Adulyadej, in 1956 donned the saffron robes of monkhood for several weeks. The King must know and practice the teachings of Buddha since it is he who is the protector of Buddhism.

A few minutes before six, I approached the Abbot's guti to watch several meditators take off their shoes at the doorstep and disappear inside. I gathered my courage, and once again tapped off my sandals and, bending low, entered.

The meditators were not gathering in the room where I had earlier met the Abbot, but in an adjoining room which resembled an office with chairs and a big modern desk which dominated the room. The females were sitting on the right and the males on the left. I slipped into the only vacant chair only to find that it was higher than the others, making me stick out like the newcomer I was.

To try to subdue my uneasiness, I took out my little notebook and began to record my impressions.

One shabbily dressed, tall and skinny youthful Western man. Four monks sitting rigidly with downcast eyes. Three of the monks are farangs; one oriental. All heads newly shaven. Farang monks look strange. Noses too big, skin too light, bodies too hairy.

Great silence. Only the rustle of vegetation tousled by the evening breeze. Desk overwhelms room. Heaps of artistic arrangements of roses, orchids, ginger, and jasmine on the desk. White and purple predominate for flowers given to the Abbot, not orange and red as I brought. Strong smell of jasmine.

Oriental monk must be meditating. Hands folded in lap, eyes half-closed, only the whites of his eyes showing. Incredible how much his eyes look like the half-open eyes of Buddha statues. It doesn't appear that he's breathing.

The silence and my attention were broken by the appearance of two young temple boys dressed in khaki shorts and white shirts. They brought two trays of yellow Chinese tea cups emblazoned with dramatic blue Chinese characters. I assumed the cups held tea, but I could not see because they were topped with lids.

Each meditator took a cup and held it, but no one drank. Neither did I. The boys departed. Silence returned.

Almost simultaneously, the monks and lay-meditators placed their tea cups on open window ledges or on the floor while I continued to hold mine, wishing that I did not have it.

As I struggled with my teacup and notebook, the Abbot walked in. The monks stood and wai-ed as he edged past them. Some of the lay-meditators stood also and everyone wai-ed to the Abbot, except me, of course, who still held a hot cup of Chinese tea in one hand and a pen and notebook in the other.

The Abbot sank behind the immense desk and silence ensued. Everyone seemed to be looking at the Abbot, but he wasn't looking back. It was as if he were not in the room, but somewhere else. I was afraid to move, but I had to get rid of the tea cup. Finally, I took courage and carefully leaned over and stuck it under my chair.

After what seemed to be ten minutes of silence, I noticed the Abbot's face beginning to twitch – just as it had done earlier in the day. Then he spoke, softly and haltingly in English with long, long pauses. I sensed that it was difficult for him to speak English. As he talked, I entered the following in my notebook.

You should learn what the Buddha taught. Buddha taught that life is 'dukkha' – suffering or unsatisfactoriness – caused by wanting, desire, craving, clinging, grasping. Birth, illness, old age, and death are dukkha.

He taught that 'sukkha' – happiness or lack of suffering – is the elimination of all desires, including the desire to cling to life itself.

He taught 'anicca' – impermanence – a constant decaying and changing that is common to all things. You, the moon, this desk, all things are changing constantly. Happiness does not come from liking or not liking things which are impermanent.

To see all this, Buddha taught us to meditate – to clear our minds, to abandon the bad and develop the good. To do that we must purify and develop our minds. That can be done through meditation.

For example – sound. Think what the mind is doing. Hear the boys playing outside. Think what the mind is doing; it's hearing.

We must develop mindfulness, 'sati'. Sati is memory – opposite of forgetting; it is to be awake – opposite of sleep; it is to know, to comprehend – opposite of ignorance.

The truth comes from one's self. One's self is the big book.

When the Abbot looked in the direction of the monks, they responded in unison with a wai and bowed their heads until he looked away.

There followed another long pause. Again it was as though he wasn't in the room. His brown skin seemed warm against the subtle saffron of his robes – the man and his robes merged.

Then he began again, so softly.

We must develop mindfulness. To develop mindfulness, or sati, we must concentrate on air, our breathing, to get the feeling or knowing of sati. In this manner we should have memory – mindfulness.

There are four places to fix the mind : 1) body 2) feeling 3) mind 4) phenomena. Use these to develop the mind, to make it mindful.

I wrote it all down, but I had little understanding. I was too shy to ask a question. After another lengthy silence, he spoke again and I recorded :

Breathing – be aware of the air touching your nostrils as it passes in and out. For beginners, it helps to count. One for the in-breath and two on the out-breath. Or count one-in and one-out, then two-in and two-out. Count up to ten breaths and then begin counting again from one.

Be mindful, but don't force your mind. When it wanders gently bring it back to being mindful on your breathing. Be patient.

Body – sit in a half-lotus position or with legs folded. Be certain to have a comfortable position. Use a cushion if necessary between the buttocks and heels in Japanese fashion. Keep your back straight. Fold your hands right over left with thumbs touching. Bend the body forward and sideways to make the body comfortable. If you can't sit still for thirty minutes, it's all right, but don't disturb the others.

Another period of silence followed before a bell rang somewhere and the two temple boys appeared. The Abbot motioned his hand to the upstairs and they disappeared. It was difficult to believe that an hour had passed since I had entered this small room.

As the Abbot rose, the students wai-ed to him as he left the room. This time, I wai-ed, but felt uncomfortable because I was not certain just how to do it before this important monk or why. One farang girl, who spoke English, whispered, 'We go upstairs now to meditate in the Abbot's meditation room.'

I tagged along. We dropped our shoes at the dark door and waited until a temple boy opened the screened door and motioned us to enter. Inside it was dull dark. Eventually a pinkness pushed away the dullness as the monks began to light candles and incense at the front of the room. I searched for the girl who had whispered to me, but before I could locate her, a young man handed me a pillow. 'You might be more comfortable if you use this,' he whispered.

'No,' I replied. 'I don't need it.'

'Then sit on these little rugs,' he suggested, pulling one closer.

I suddenly realized that everyone was kneeling on the rugs, so I quickly got down on the floor. Everyone seemed to be waiting for something. All eyes were on the Abbot and the monks who were sitting in front of an altar in the front portion of the room. The room seemed to have two distinct sections; one for the religious and one for lay people.

As those in the saffron robes began prostrating themselves three times before the Buddha image, the meditators joined in. I remained rigid in a kneeling position, watching. After prostration, everyone manoeuvred himself into a lotus or half-lotus position. I kept my eyes on the girl in front of me – trying to duplicate her every movement.

One temple boy entered and turned on an overhead fan of Somerset Maugham vintage, then plugged in a small electric fan, pointing it so that it blew directly on the lay meditators. As the first breeze passed over me, I was glad, for not only would this gentle breeze relieve some of the evening's oppressive heat, but it might prevent most mosquitoes from sampling my blood.

Prior to departing for the wat, not knowing that there would be fans in the wat, I had doused myself heavily with Sketolene, a powerful Asian mosquito repellent.

Finally I manoeuvred my legs and body into a tolerable half-lotus position. I was glad that my loose dress didn't seem to touch my body anywhere. Its fullness gave me sufficient room to sit cross-legged in a modest fashion. I reminded myself always to wear something too big for me when I came here.

At last I seemed ready to begin. Mind on my breath, I began bringing in large amounts of air. I could tell that my breathing was abnormal, but it was interesting to feel the air, cool and tingling rush along the hair follicles inside my nose. Now to be mindful – to concentrate on nothing but the air coming in and coming out. I started to count – one – in, one – out; two – in. Then my mind was gone. It skipped to the powerful smell of the mosquito repellent, then it jumped to wonder if there would be mosquitoes in my room tonight, and then flitted to review my afternoon meeting with the Abbot. I started to count again – and again – and again. But each time my mind escaped, to rapidly climb a mounting thought only to flit to another, or to touch on a past event, or to stop to rest momentarily on a really stupid, mundane episode like the taxi driver who overcharged me.

This made me nervous. I could not hold my mind still for even a matter of seconds. Then I remembered the Abbot's words of warning, 'Don't force it. When your mind wanders, gently bring it back.' Maybe I was trying too hard. If I could only relax. But I could not. It was such a new experience for me and for some reason I seemed to be very emotional about beginning this adventure.

Finally I gave up the struggle and opened my eyes. I looked at my watch. About fifteen minutes had passed. The other meditators remained motionless in the dim light. The Abbot was no longer there, but the four younger monks were still meditating, immobile.

As my eyes became accustomed to the soft light, I noticed beautiful Chinese-style porcelain bowls and plates displayed in ornate cabinets along the walls. I wondered about their origins. Monks were not supposed to own anything. Later I discovered that the faithful had donated them to the wat – a way to make merit, to do a good deed.

Deep red and maroon coloured rugs, with intricate designs, which the monks were sitting on, appeared to be Persian.

I slowly moved my hand to touch the floor; it was cool, hard, and, made of teak. The candles sputtered dramatically in the man-made breeze sending erratic tongues of light over the silent monks and the image of a sitting Buddha atop the altar. No matter where the flickering light fell on the image's face – whether the eyes, nose, or mouth, there was a sense of restfulness or tranquillity or was it peace?

Smouldering incense defied the flopping fan to hang heavy in the air. It smelled good – or was it the jasmine flowers adorning the altar that piqued my senses.

This room was becoming friendly.

After another twenty minutes, meditators began to stir – very slowly at first, maybe only the lifting of a head or the moving of an arm. Then they began shifting their sitting positions. I sat very still, pretending my eyes were closed, mainly because I did not know what was to happen next.

The monks came to life slowly. One by one they prostrated themselves three times in front of the Buddha image. Soon the lay meditators did the same.

Quietly, and without any pomp, the lay meditators arose and tip-toed out to the door to search in the dimness for their shoes. With their shoes on, they walked away silently into the darkness. No words had been spoken. I followed, but a bit more slowly. My right leg had fallen asleep.

I limped out of the quietness of the wat compound into the noise of traffic and the din of a Chinese cloth market, and headed for my room, several blocks away. I wanted to think about the past two hours, but it was too noisy. Later, as I walked down my dimly lit lane, the sweet smells from the flower market oozed out into the tropical night air reminding me of the jasmine smell in the Abbot's guti and I began to wonder if I would *ever* be able to hold my mind still past the count of two? I was doubtful.

Besides, in the past I had always found it most exhilarating to allow my mind to roam wildly. Some of my best ideas came when my mind raced like the wind through and over myriads of recollections, images, and fantasies. Did I really want to change all this?

As I walked the final dark yards to my room, I reflected on the evening. Suddenly, I realized that the whole class had been directed to me. The Abbot had obviously gone back to the beginning precepts of meditation – just for me, the newcomer. A rush of warm feeling for this man came over me. 'I must try,' I whispered to myself as I unlocked the door. 'I must practise his instructions again and again.'

I sat down on the floor in the darkness of my room and began to try to be mindful of my breathing. I began counting – one-in, one-out; two-in. I began over and over – one-in, one-out; two-in – And thus it went for almost an hour, although I never legitimately went beyond 'two' without my mind rebelling from the task at hand.

Tired and disillusioned, I crawled into bed. Across the floor, moonlight, distorted by the heavy tropical vegetation, danced in fleeting images – as did my mind.

# Chapter Two

Meditation is not something that was invented in –
and happened in – history. It is an ageless human
experience that has been discovered and explored
and used in every period and every culture . . .

Lawrence Leshan.
*How To Meditate*

I awoke the next few mornings thinking of the Abbot and
the special consideration which he was giving me, the beginner, at the dhamma classes. These pleasant thoughts seemed
to prompt me to slip from my bed each morning to try again
to practise mindfulness of breathing.

Each day it became easier to get into a comfortable half-
lotus sitting position and it seemed easier to concentrate on my
breathing. The counting had advanced to four, sometimes even
five, without interruptions, but most of the time I managed
only a count of three.

This morning I practised for twenty-five minutes; it was
considerably more relaxed than previous sessions, which was
encouraging, but I was still apprehensive. Why was I unable to
hold my mind still for anything more than a mere dot in time?
I had always thought that I had control over my mind. So why
couldn't I do this seemingly simple exercise. Why not? Then
I recalled the familiar warning that was repeated so often at
Wat Bovornives. 'Don't force meditation; be patient.'

Placated by the thought that there still might be hope for
me, I decided that today was the day to explore the stack of
books on Buddhism which had been given to me by a Thai
lady who was steeped in Buddhist philosophy. As I looked
through the stack, I realized that I was familiar with only one
book. I felt very ignorant and humble.

I had experienced this same feeling earlier when this lady
had informed me that a popular Western book on Buddhism
that I had with me was no good, misleading, and incorrect.
This morning I pushed that book far beneath my bed and
turned to the new books, written in English and published in
either Sri Lanka or Thailand by Buddhists.

I read until noon. Then, inspired undoubtedly by the small success in the morning's meditation, I tried mindfulness of breathing again for another thirty minutes. The results were not much different from the morning, but now it seemed more natural.

In the evening I decided not to use the counting system but to be mindful of the in-breath and the out-breath – by thinking breathing-in and breathing-out. This method seemed more suitable for me.

After this practice, I sat alone in my small room reflecting on the past days, the results of which I entered in my meditation notebook.

A routine has developed for me which changes little day to day. There are dhamma and meditation classes at Wat Bovornives and Buddhist writings to read. There are discussions on Buddhism with friends and lay scholars at other wats, particularly Wat Sraket.

While my physical world changes little with each passing day, I'm becoming aware that something quite new and different is beginning to take place within me. But I'm not certain I understand it.

A few days later I entered another synopsis of my progress.

I practise mindfulness of breathing three times a day – early morning, early afternoon, and evening. At first the sessions lasted approximately twenty-five to thirty minutes. Now the length of time is increasing, but not by any conscious effort on my part. It appears to be a natural occurrence as it becomes easier and easier for me to become mindful of my breathing.

I have abandoned the counting system as not the proper method for me. My mind still has its fits of skittering about uncontrollably, but, unlike the initial days, I don't try to force my mind. Each time it wanders, I gently acknowledge to what it has roamed and then bring it back to being aware of my breathing.

There are bouts with pain and mosquitoes. I don't always

meditate where there are fans to keep the mosquitoes away nor does the mosquito repellent always fend them off successfully. If only I weren't allergic to their bites.

Then there is the problem of my leg going to sleep and the itches and scratches that are so disconcerting in meditation. The monks told me that when pain occurs to think 'paining, paining, paining' and it will go away, or when a mosquito is biting to think the same, or if it is a matter of an itch, to concentrate on the itch and repeat mentally, 'itching, itching, itching'. Previously I have always thought that if one could ignore the source of irritation or pain it would go away. But here I am being told to become more aware of it, to try to see the nature of it, to concentrate on the irritation or pain itself. I have been doubting that this method will work since mosquito bites usually give me hives, so tonight I will test the theory.

While meditating in the Abbot's guti, the left side of my nose began to twitch and itch mercilessly. My mind seemed uncontrollable; there seemed to be no way that I could keep my attention on the breathing when this itch seemed to be spreading over my entire face. So, hesitantly and very skeptically, I allowed my mind to switch completely to the itch.

My mind became aware of the itch with great energy. I wanted desperately to scratch, but I held back, repeating 'itching, itching, itching'. The itching continued to spread. Again I concentrated on 'itching, itching, itching' for what seemed a long time. Then it stopped!

As soon as the nose itching ceased, there came a strong itch beneath my left breast; one that couldn't be ignored. I allowed my mind to flow there and settle on the discomfort while I slowly repeated, 'itching, itching, itching'. I repeated it again and then again. Finally that discomfort was eliminated.

Then an itch on my right side sprang up. This was ridiculous! But I followed the instructions. This time the words had to be repeated only once, but very slowly and with full concentration.

I'm not certain I understand any of this, but it seems possible to eliminate pain with powerful concentration.

Pains and itches continued to trouble me in meditation, but I refused to give in to them. I neither rubbed nor scratched. There were other problems that also interfered with meditation.

For several days, I was aware only of my breath coming in. I could not feel it coming out, which was most disturbing. Sometimes it felt as if my body, puffed up with all the inhaled air, would explode.

One evening after dhamma class, I reported the problem. A monk in attendance told me that I was not being mindful or aware. 'Of course, the air is coming out. If you were more aware you would be able to distinguish the change in temperature of the air that entered your nose and that being released.'

Again he reminded me not to force breathing because it was a form of desire or grasping and that I was too anxious for success in meditation. He was undoubtedly right. I probably was obsessed with the 'I' or 'self' – because *I* wanted to succeed; *I* wanted to be a good meditator. It was true that *I* was determined to absorb all I could about Buddhism and meditation. The monk was right. *I wanted* too much and it was destroying or, at least, hindering my practice.

I knew that to eliminate the 'I want' frame of reference I would have to become more relaxed – to be a participant in the middle-way, a way that recommends no over-indulgence nor extreme asceticism.

That evening, after the discussion, the class went to the Abbot's meditation room. This room was becoming a more friendly room for me partly because I knew the routine of the dhamma and meditation classes and partly because the fear of making a grand 'faux pas' was subsiding. Yet I was still edgy about the three wai before and after meditation. The exact procedures involved in making the wai and the reason for it remained a mystery. My resolution of the problem was to wai once, keeping my head to the floor until the others had finished this ceremony.

Sitting in the soothing atmosphere, I reflected on what had transpired thus far in my meditation, trying to prepare myself to begin all over again – to try to be more mindful – to develop sati. Samadhi, or concentration meditation as this form of meditation was called, no longer remained unknowable. I was beginning to understand something of the theory of sati; it seemed to be an attempt to teach the meditator to develop or control his mind so that he could reach some state of tranquillity.

However, I was finding great pain or suffering in the bouncing and leaping about of my mind as I tried to be aware of my breathing. I could physically feel my mind jumping from side to side, to and fro, and then back again in ridiculous fleeting bounds that seemed to lead nowhere. My mind was a muscle, twisting, pulling and leaping. Its actions resembled muscular cramps that twitch on and on uncontrollably. Never before had I been aware of the mind's apparent physical energies.

I could not comprehend the depths of samadhi meditation, but, knowing that man has learned to use only a very small portion of his mind and now learning that man could be taught to expand his mind's range and abilities through the techniques of samadhi meditation, I began thinking that meditation could be a most desirable activity.

After all these thoughts had paraded through my mind, I settled into a comfortable position and began breathing-in and breathing-out. It seemed much easier now that I had accepted that I must start from the beginning.

My most recent problem seemed to be gone; my breath was flowing both ways. As the breathing-in and breathing-out became soft and routine, I became aware of a mass of amorphous grey putty that was hanging under my nose, or maybe it was between my eyes, I was not certain. Eventually I became aware that this was my mind! There it hung, outside of my head, congealed together in a most unattractive manner. The breathing-in and breathing-out continued rhythmically while the conglomerate of unknown textures floated about. It seemed as if my mind were there and not there at the same time. I acknowledged a force of concentrated energy in it, yet it seemed ethereal in that it wasn't anything that had a recognizable form.

It seemed as if there were, at least, two minds; one concentrating on the breathing and the other one looking at the greyish mass. The bulbous form was there, but recessed, as if it were on another plane, while the breathing was taking place on the same plane that I was on.

The bulb shimmered and moved about in fleeting movements, becoming dark grey and then lighter grey. It remained while I continued to be aware of both the breathing and my mind hanging outside my head. The intrigue of this configuration, heavy with energy, finally pulled my complete attention to it, or so it seemed. When I concentrated on it directly to have a good scientific look, it disappeared. I returned to breathing-in and breathing-out, but it failed to reappear.

42

Then, seemingly without any suggestion from me, the meditation seemed to be ending. Concentration on my breathing began to wane, and a soft, fragile feeling followed. I wanted to keep my eyes closed, to keep the meditation going, yet I knew that it was over. I had to make a conscious effort to open my eyes and to move my hands. It was difficult to move, yet there was awareness that it must be done.

I looked at my watch, which I always placed on the floor beside me since I didn't like anything touching me during meditation; I had been sitting in meditation for forty-five minutes while it seemed that only five or ten had passed.

I remained sitting on the little saffron rug for some time. There was a feeling of quietness both in the room and in myself that was a new experience. It felt good and I rejoiced in this feeling – which was undoubtedly wrong for I was 'clinging' to something again. It was the first time that I had been aware of this kind of delicate quietness.

Then I became aware that I was alone except for a temple boy who was peeping at me from an adjoining room. I supposed he was waiting for me to leave so that he could turn off the fans.

It seemed that my meditation practice was progressing, although slowly. Yet I was constantly reminded by meditation instructors and from readings that a meditator who worries about his progress is caught by delusion and greed and these defilements will prevent him from practising satisfactorily.

One evening in the Abbot's guti, not long after the appearance of the grey amorphous mass hanging somewhere under my nose, a new experience unfolded. I did not understand why new directions always seemed to take place first in the Abbot's meditation room. Was it because of the inspiration of dhamma class prior to meditation, the inspiration of the Abbot himself sitting in meditation before me, or the atmosphere of this room which seemed·so conducive to meditation? Or what?

This particular meditation session began in the usual way: getting comfortable, making certain that no clothes were binding my body; taking off my watch; getting my left leg as comfortable as possible since it inevitably went to sleep; straightening my back and body so that my body seemed to be firmly supported by my legs and buttocks. I was much more comfortable with the breathing awareness exercises now. It was becoming easier and easier to still the mind and for longer periods of time. In fact, meditation was something that I, in the past days, had come to welcome.

This night, the breathing-in and breathing-out brought with it a pin prick of blue ever so tiny. This pin prick of blue was in infinity, far, far away. It flickered and grew larger until it filled my horizons. It spread and grew to unlimited proportions. The original colour changed into multitudes of various intensities and shades of blue, ranging from deep purples to the lightest of aquas. Like a gigantic kaleidoscope, the patterned colours twisted, turned, increased, and diminished in a swirl of exquisite shapes, designs and shades.

The breathing remained close to me and dominant. The kaleidoscoping colours and patterns remained distant, beyond me – free, undulating, creating, moving at rapid speeds tumbling throughout entire universes. The colours played and danced in an infinite distance just beyond my reach, yet, I was aware of an exhilaration in this beauty. I seemed, however, to be afraid to release my mind from the breathing-in and breathing-out.

Later, I wondered how it was possible to be aware of the

breathing process and at the same time to be aware of infinite fields of colours? How many minds did I have? How does perception take place in the mind?

For some days to come, my meditation seemed invariably to include psychedelic displays which began with a minute speck in a huge vastness. Sometimes the speck was a tiny, very intense light, piercingly brilliant, from which evolved a massive amount of bluish colour that flowed out and captivated an entire universe, bringing me joy from the beauty of its art. Often at the beginning of meditation, the grey bulb – what seemed to be my mind – would appear somewhere beneath my nose, holding within its elusive shape a sense of energy.

Then, one day, before the colour parade began, the energy mass which was usually light grey took on a tinge of yellow, a glowing yellow, almost luminous. It wavered and jumped evasively. At times it seemed very near, or was it the fact that its amorphous nature seemed to be taking more detailed shapes and forms which, perhaps, made it seem closer?

Although it continued to quiver and wiggle, a design was forming. One that I could not absolutely recognize. Once it seemed to be the shape of a small Buddhist charm that many Thais wear around their necks for good fortune. Another time it seemed to be the silhouette of a Buddha sitting in a meditating position. And another time it took a shape resembling the unfolding of a lotus blossom.

It continued to appear in mystifying forms and I often wondered what it was. Did it have any meaning? Probably not, I decided, but why was it so persistent? Why did this attractive, luminescent image try to lure the engagement of my concentration? I thought it might pass in time, but it did not.

Then, one night during an after-meditation discussion session, although I was still shy about my ignorance of meditation, I asked why my meditation was accompanied by blues. Why not other colours?

The presiding monk, a young man of about twenty-five, did not have an explanation, but turned the question around a bit. 'What do you do with the blue colours?'

'Nothing,' I answered. 'I enjoy them and try to be mindful of my breathing.'

'It's dukkha to enjoy them,' he reminded me. 'You are liking and wanting the colours. Do not become attached to them. Since blue is considered a calming colour, the next time, instead of enjoying the colours, try pulling them into your body through your breathing.'

Almost as a footnote, he added, 'But you shouldn't do that with the "nimitta". You should ignore it.'

I didn't understand his warning because I didn't know the word, nimitta. Thinking it was probably a stupid question, I gathered courage to ask what he meant by nimitta.

'Nimitta is a symbol or shape, a visual image, that often appears at some point in meditation. It's often called an acquired sign. This sign seems to be different for each person, but,' the monk explained in a soft voice, 'it indicates a calming or stilling of the mind. When a nimitta is developing, concentration is beginning to work.

'Remember that the nimitta is not *yours* nor *you*. The coming and disappearing of the nimitta, like all impermanent things, exemplifies impermanence, which is a cause of suffering or dukkha. The nimitta comes and goes as conditions arise or cease; it is the result of causes and effects. Don't be a slave to the nimitta. The beauty should not be in the nimitta but in the fact that the mind is relatively calm and tranquil

'Concentration,' he continued, 'is the key to meditation, but meditation must always be on the immediate present. Be careful of the nimitta because it can be extremely powerful. Be alert to it. Remember, do not become enslaved to it!'

He concluded by suggesting that if I would come by his guti, he would give me a book in English that explained the nimitta in detail.

On my long walk home, I wondered about the monk's warning on the dangers of attachment to a nimitta. I did not understand what he meant, so I decided that it would be wise to follow his advice and read about this phenomenon.

The next day I borrowed the monk's book and found the following explanation of nimitta written by one of Thailand's leading, though highly controversial Buddhist intellectuals, a monk named Buddhadasa.

In a discussion on the steps involved in learning mindfulness of breathing, he wrote that the first step is to become aware of how long or how short the breath is and where the centre of the breath seems to be. The second step involves fixing the mind on the gate, or nostrils. In this second step, the breathing, he concluded, should be soft and calm. Next he discussed the nimitta and I copied a passage from his book into my diary.

When the Acquired Sign, (the nimitta) is well-maintained, it tends to be still, and the mind is calmed down. After this the Acquired Sign begins to change in shape. How big or small it appears or how beautiful it is or where it is placed, is different to different individuals. For example, to some this mental image appears as something white right in front of their face, or as a huge moon in the sky or on the top of a tree or in the nostril; this depends on individuals and their slightest idiosyncracies which are more or less automatic. But, finally, after having taken some particular shape and place, this mental image becomes invariable without the least change.*

I was fascinated by all this. Did this mean that I was making some progress? Was this repeating image a nimitta? Undoubtedly it was. But the most interesting part of it all was that I had not known about nimitta until after it had occurred in my own meditation.

But why should I be alert to its powers? I read on and recorded the following.

This is the stage (of the Acquired Sign) where mind, like a well-tamed monkey, becomes peaceful and calm. One feels showered with bliss owing to pervasion by the feeling of happiness. One can notice Applied and Sustained Thoughts, Rapture, Happiness, and One-pointedness being present in complete harmony with the mind . . . This is the stage in

* *'Towards Buddha-Dhamma'*, Buddhadasa Bhikkhu, p. 32-33. by Siripat Co, Bangkok, Thailand

which we have the 'patibhaga-nimitta', the Absorption Sign. The moment we arrive at this stage, the mind is completely freed from the unwholesome mental objects which are technically called the five 'nirvanas' (mental hindrances, namely, lust, ill-will, torpor and sloth, restlessness and mental worry, and doubt).*

The word absorption startled me. I thought of absorption in connection with yogas and trance states which I understood to be periods of extraordinarily powerful concentration. I knew that I did not have to worry about reaching any state of absorption, not if it meant being free of restlessness, worry, doubt. I had enough of these qualities to last a life-time.

What was the danger of a nimitta? Was it allowing the nimitta to become an unchecked source of power for concentration so that all else was eliminated?

It was interesting to speculate on all this, but I felt that it was something with which I would never have to be concerned.

In meditation the next evening, my breathing was soft and calm. It was so much easier to be mindful of my breathing now. The nimitta appeared with its quaking and shimmering luminous outlines along with the omnipresent blues. In a kind of modern abstract painting of chromatic colours, the dark blues at the bottom expanded into lighter and lighter blues, rounding off with the most delicate of light blues.

As recommended, instead of enjoying the colours or becoming attached to them, I attempted to pull them into my body with my breathing as I slowly, calmly, and somewhat languidly breathed-in and breathed-out. The colours easily came toward me, but I wasn't aware of them actually entering my body, though I could see them coming in, in a flowing stream to the call of my breathing. At the point where they touched my nose, I became unaware of them. At moments, it seemed that I was aware of the nimitta, the breathing, and

* *Ibid.*, p. 33.

48

the flowing, restful blueness. I could not consume all the blueness; there was always a universe more to be drawn in.

Then slowly, so slowly, the blues receded and swirled away down a pin prick hole. I was mindful only of breathing and tranquillity and then a knowing that meditation was ceasing.

The cessation of meditation is intriguing. It all happens so naturally, yet there is a distinct longing for it to continue. There is a sense of joy in meditating, there's an anticipation for more of it with its resulting joy. All of which is undoubtedly bad since meditation seeks to lead one to develop the mind to the levels where wanting of any kind is completely extinguished.

This sense of joy and calmness remained with me after meditation. As I headed home through the noisy and crowded market streets, I felt so light that I was certain that I would faint before reaching my room. I did not, though this buoyant feeling remained for several hours.

From the beginning days of meditation practice, I found it impossible to eat after meditating. Sometimes I would drink a glass of water, iced-tea, or some fruit juice, but tonight I could not force myself to drink anything. Later, I discovered that this is a common experience among meditators.

Often, after coming from the wat, I would sit on my bed, sometimes sipping a cool drink and ponder meditation. This night was no exception. As I thought about the relative ease with which I had entered tonight's meditation and the calmness that followed, I recalled the warnings of knowledgeable friends . . . 'Don't be deluded by thinking that you are making progress in meditation and in the understanding of dhamma. Meditation is a long and painful process. There are no short-cuts. Never!'

I knew these warnings were valid. Yet tonight, while I was meditating, it seemed that I was able to be mindful on my breathing, to be aware of the nimitta and the blues, and, at the same time, to be aware of the temple dogs barking and temple boys playing.

As it occurred, I recorded in my mind that I was hearing dogs and boys, but it was a neutral recording. I was conscious of them, but not distracted. Was this a kind of detachment?

I began to think about the troublesome Buddhist concept of detachment and the four qualities of 'metta' or loving kindness, of 'karuna' or compassion, of 'mudita' or sympathetic joy and of 'upekkha' or equanimity. I understood that if we cultivated these qualities then we would know something of a higher level of being.

Worrying about the seeming conflict between detachment and these four qualities, I wrote in my notebook.

Is detachment being aware of all things but not relating or reacting to them – an acknowledgement but no involvement? But if I don't relate, how can I show loving kindness or metta. The monks always speak of developing metta. It seems a basic and simple meditation goal, but how can I extend loving kindness, without any delusions or pretensions, to *everybeing* – whether human, animal, or insect. This is no easy task. Experiencing metta might be easier than knowing the other three so-called divine abidings or sublime states of consciousness of compassion, joy or gladness, and equanimity. These are words that I thought were familiar to me for often I write about love, joy, and compassion. But the compassion, joy, and equanimity of Buddhism are strangers to me. According to Buddhist theories, these qualities, to be pure, have to exist without attachment. I can not understand how compassion can be compassion if it has to exist without attachment.

## Chapter Three

Man, even in this life, is never the same, yet ever
the result of his pre-existing life.

G. P. Malalasekera
Aspects of Reality as Taught by Theravada Buddhism.


DURING the time that I was studying dhamma and meditation
with the Abbot at Wat Bovornives, I was also studying Buddhist philosophy with a lay scholar at Wat Sraket in Bangkok.
A Thai lady, herself a Buddhist scholar, had arranged this for
me.

Wat Sraket is famous for its Golden Mountain, a massive
gilt structure that winds upward in ever-decreasing spirals to
loom majestically over the city of Bangkok. Actually, the
Golden Mountain is a 'chedi', a funerary reportedly enshrining
some of the Buddha's bones. From the top of this golden
structure, one can see all the city of Bangkok and beyond to
the never-ending rice fields that drift into shimmering heat
waves and hazy skies. I only rarely climbed the Golden
Mountain; I came to Wat Sraket to study with a Thai gentle-
man who spoke English well and, among his many tasks,
conducted small classes for Thais in the study of 'Abhidhamma', the philosophical tracts of Buddhism.

Each time I ascended the steps to the large, sprawling hall
in the Wat Sraket compound where the instructions were
given, I felt a tingle. It seemed as though when I entered this
hall, shoeless and humble, I was walking into the past. The
shiny, smooth teak floor of this teaching hall was cool and
ageless beneath my feet. Each day a breeze met me – a breeze
that seemed to exist only in this building. I often wondered
how it could be so cool and quiet, when only yards away
hectic traffic, pollution, and heat were savage. A wat always
seemed a haven from the world, no matter where it was
located.


Her head was shaved; she wore white. She was a Buddhist

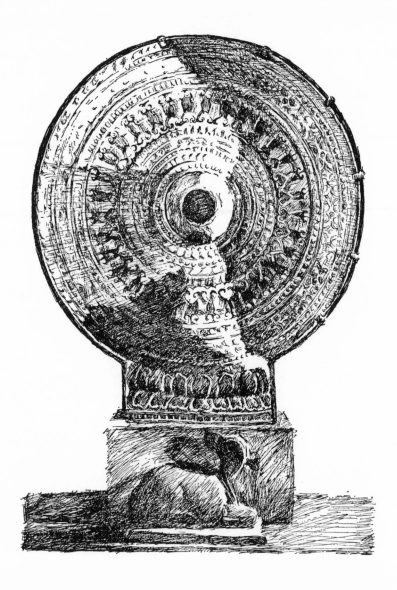

nun. Each day as she saw me coming up the stairs, she would disappear behind a white cotton screen in one corner. As soon as I was seated at a little instruction table, this diminutive young woman would reappear holding with both hands a glass of water, tinted pink, scented, and covered with a lid. Her greeting was accompanied by a smile that I've seen etched on the face of many Buddha statues. 'Bhikkhuni', orders of female monks originated in the time of Buddha, had died out centuries ago, so she was called a 'mae-chee' and she assisted in the wat with cooking, marketing, tending to flowers, or attending to lay people, like myself, who came to the wat to study. I later learned that there is an effort in Thailand to elevate the status of the nun.

Usually I had to wait a few minutes for the scholar to finish his other work which often involved the overseeing of two young people who were recording Pali chants on a tape recorder. I loved these minutes by myself. These chants in Pali, the ancient Indic language of the Buddhist scriptures, resounded with the full tremor of orchestras of kettle drums. As I waited, I often thought about the Buddha. It was stimulating, yet difficult to remember that Buddha was a man – never a god, or creator, or judge. He was a sage of the profoundest wisdom. It was a joy to know that Buddha, since he was merely a man – a great teacher nonetheless – who lived over 2,500 years ago could not cast down his wrath on me or any other being. He would not punish me for wrong-doing nor save me. The Buddha held no such powers. There could be no intervention from the heavens, therefore prayers to him would be useless. I did not have to renounce anything to practise his teachings or to learn of his meditation. Buddha's teachings were a path to follow. It is said that the Buddha again and again stressed that one should not accept his teachings with blind faith but examine them with reason.

Whenever I thought about these things, a sense of freedom seemed to permeate my being.

I was responsible for myself. These were pleasant things to think about. Yet I sensed that for many Buddhists, Buddha was conceived of as a godhead who was worshipped by rituals, ceremonies, and idols. These followers had forgotten that he was a man, a teacher, perfected by his own wisdom – a wisdom which every being was supposedly capable of attaining.

Eventually, the scholar, a middle-aged Thai who had spent years studying Buddhist writings, would finish his tasks and come to our little table to sit opposite me – the eager student who waited with notebook and pen ready to take notes. I would go with this man, with the round face and intelligent eyes, into the past to ponder the teachings of the Indian Prince who, after years of contemplation, self-denial, and searching, came upon an understanding of the nature of human life. From these insights, he formulated teachings which became both a philosophy and a code of ethics – a way of life.

Initially the most difficult thing to understand was the scholar's explanation that the results of man's past deeds could cause his rebirth into one of thirty-one different regions or worlds. He told me that some of these thirty-one kinds of life man could see – such as the animal class, insect class, and the human class; but there were other classes of life that man could not see.

The teacher continued to explain that human beings are considered to be the standard class with four lower forms and twenty-six higher. Sometimes, the beings from the demon and spirit classes would allow man to see them. Various classes of beings existed in worlds reserved for those with a high degree of spiritual development. The elite class of these beings, referred to by the Thai as the 'phroom' class, is an historical reference to Bhrahama, a supreme Hindu god, who was not deposed by Buddhism, but instead relegated to a lesser status. The idea of the existence of other worlds and universes fascinated me. It seemed basically in this context that some Buddhists explain other religions.

I was intrigued by the calmness with which the Buddhists accept other religions. For them it is not a question of there being only one God, for to them there is no God, no Ultimate Creator nor Destroyer. There is no threat to them from a

Jesus or Mohammed. Some Thais, it seems, understand that these great men were advanced and highly developed in terms of their kamma, and had known life in the world of the phroom. Jesus and Mohammed were good, wise men, but there lies beyond a state of being which they did not yet know – nibbana, where suffering is unknown.

The Thai Buddhist does not believe that reaching the phroom state, which in literary descriptions sometimes resembles the heaven of Christianity, is an ultimate goal, because even in these highest of existences there will be eventual rebirth and more suffering. There is only the attainment of nibbana where there is freedom from rebirth.

My teacher explained that what happened to the beings in the phroom class happened to all beings. There was no escape from rebirth until the attainment of nibbana. All beings would continue on the ceaseless cycle of birth-and-death to be born again and again. If good deeds were practised, then one might be reborn into a phroom class or into a rich family with many material good things. If less charity were practised or if evil deeds were done, then the result might be rebirth into a poor family or maybe as some lowly creature.

'Buddhism', as this scholar at Wat Sraket had explained on our first meeting, 'is a way of life. If every man in the community keeps the five precepts of Buddhism then the community will live together in peace. If no one drank fermented liquids, nor stole, nor killed, nor committed adultery, nor lied, there would be no struggle in life.

'Life is a struggle,' he continued, 'because life is based on an irrevocable moral law of cause and effect. Whatever we are is a result of our actions, thoughts, and deeds in preceding lives. We are a result of our deeds. Both good and bad deeds have effects. The effect is light or strong according to the *intention* of the deed. For example, if we kill a mosquito, the effect is much lighter than if we kill a man. Also, if a good deed is thoughtfully planned the resulting good effects are greater than a good deed done just to get rid of an obligation. Man classifies himself according to his deeds. That's why we have classes of society, even in communist countries.'

It all seemed so understandable and logical to the teacher, but I wasn't certain how anyone, by his own efforts, ever managed to cast himself free from the rebirth cycles.

All of this thinking seemed to rest on a belief in a law of cause and effect – a law that was by its nature just, righteous, and irrevocable. Because of this law, the results of a human's actions – both the good and bad deeds – must be acted out. The fruits of one's actions might not be realized in the present lifetime, but in a future life. But realized they would be – and that was kamma in operation.

I struggled with my teacher's thinking by presenting him with such obvious facts as that many people who are unscrupulous, dishonest, unjust, and often cruel become leaders who receive public acclaim and hold vast wealth. They often live long, healthy lives with no apparent retribution for their evil deeds.

Like other Theravada Buddhists, his beliefs in this just law seemed indomitable. To illustrate his point, he used American history.

'President Kennedy suffered his terrible misfortune for some bad deed that he had committed maybe 100,000 lives ago. And the original Mr Rockefeller, who struck oil, was receiving the result of good deeds done in previous lives.'

I often thought about this supposedly irrevocable law of justice which prompted me to write in my notebook:

Isn't it more logical, this irrevocable law of cause and effect, than the belief that a man – a bad man, even a derelict, murderer, swindler, slaver who intentionally harms others for his own aggrandizement – can after all these evil deeds, be 'saved', which means that his past evil actions disappear as if they never occurred?

According to this scholar,

'To understand the teachings of Buddha takes a long time and it takes right understanding. You must understand that there is a common quality among all beings and things whether they be demon, spirit, insect, millionaire, phroom, mountain, or empire. That common quality is *impermanence*, 'anicca', a constant decaying and changing which is uncontrollable. It is this impermanence and man's insistence on liking and disliking, wanting and not wanting these things that causes suffering and unhappiness.'

I could easily understand the erosion, decay, and changing features of a mountain, but when he told me that because everything is constantly changing, including me, then there is no constant 'I' or 'self', I found this thinking so foreign that I had great difficulty in managing the concept.

I troubled over this until I found an explanation by Alexander Griswold that made sense and I wrote it in my study notebook.

It (Buddha Dhamma) maintains that no individual – whether animal, man, or god (if gods exist) – is permanent. Each is a compound, a putting together, of elements such as form, matter, and mental qualities; in each individual, without any exception, the relation of component parts, constantly changing, is never the same for any two consecutive moments. No sooner has separateness, individuality begun, than dissolution, disintegration begins, too.*

With the impermanence problem somewhat solved, I soon had to deal with others such as suffering, its causes, and its cessation.

This scholar at Wat Sraket explained that the Buddha taught that unsatisfactoriness, unhappiness, or suffering was a cause and inevitable truth of life, but that there was a way to eliminate the causes which created suffering. Suffering, so the Buddha taught, was caused by such things as greed, hatred and ignorance, particularly ignorance of the impermanence of all things. If these causes could be eliminated then suffering would be eliminated.

My mentor continued to reinforce the notion that greed – our desires, our wants to gain, our wants not to lose what we

* Alexander B. Griswold, 'King Mongkut in Perspective', *Journal Siam Society*, XLV (1957) p. 16-18.

have, our keen desire to cling to life itself – provides the impetus which leads to rebirths as unhappy and filled with suffering as they may be. 'It is this greed – this grasping and clinging – that holds us within the cycle wheel of life to be reborn again and again. The Buddha taught that when the causes which create suffering are eliminated, then we will be cast free of the rebirth cycle, not to suffer again. Suffering, when it is no longer caused, will be absent and rebirth will not occur. Then we will be free from birth-and-death. It is freedom; it is nibbana.'

Of the many things that puzzled me, I was most uncertain about the Theravadin concept of rebirth. I had heard a few people – very few in fact – explain the concept of rebirth not as a physical dying and rebirth, but as a rebirth of man's mind from moment to moment which could place him temporarily in various regions – anger could catapult him into a state of hell or joy could lift him to soar to a bliss similar to a phroom state. But it seemed that most Theravada Buddhists understood the concept of rebirth not as a fluctuating mental state, but as a physical rebirth after the cessation of any one particular life.

This popular belief was the one that interested me most. I wanted to know what lived on after the present body died. Was it energy? Energy generated by a man's soul, psyche, or mind? Or was it the energy of life itself that continues beyond the demise of heart, liver, or pancreas?

How much energy can a man or any living creature generate? Probably a considerable amount. Infra-red photography is used by the United States military reconnaissance planes in photographing enemy movements. Low-flying jets rigged with infra-red film can pick up and record on film the outlines or shapes through the diffusion of the heat and energy cast off by man and machine hours after both have moved on. The Buddhists speak of an energy created by our deeds and actions. Is it the same kind of energy that can be photographed? How long does this energy exist after the body has gone? Intrigued by possible similarities between the developments of technology and an ancient belief, I mused at the possibility that a tremendous amount of energy is expanded in a deed fostered by great hatred or passion.

Whatever it is that exists beyond the physical death of a body, I couldn't learn. A common answer was that it was kamma which remains with all beings forever and determines the nature of the next existence.

I was becoming aware, also, that the concept of time had a completely different orientation from the Western sense of time that is based, to a large degree, on a human lifetime of approximately seventy years.

The popular twentieth-century American attitude that 'I have only one life to live so let me fill it with as many experiences as possible,' is difficult for the Buddhist to comprehend. He believes, rather, that there are untold lives that he must endure before he will be released from the wheel of life. Maybe it is because of this belief in the endlessness and immensity of time that the Buddhist focuses on the present.

'When we live in the present,' the scholar explained, 'we can always be alert to bad thoughts and bad deeds. By developing an awareness of living in the present, we can come to know ourselves.'

I sensed that there was a corollary between the notion of impermanence of all things and the concept of being aware of the present, but I couldn't comprehend the nuances. Only later in meditation in northern Thailand would I understand, through experience, what was meant by focusing on the present, forgetting the past, and therefore influencing the future.

I pondered many things, often without finding any answers. Then one day, this scholar led me through a most intriguing set of ideas. I agreed with him that man knows his world or reality through his five senses. Then I was asked to consider if man developed his five senses to a higher degree or if he developed other senses, would he see his world or reality as he previously perceived it? The answer seemed logical . . . No. Then he proposed that if man had other senses or more developed ones, then wouldn't he probably be able to perceive other phenomena that required recognition by means other than the traditional form, sound, colour, touch, or taste? I answered, 'Yes', not knowing where this logic would take us. Then I was asked to consider that if man's means of contact with his world is so limited, because of his limited senses, then how can man know reality? How can man know that there is an 'I' or 'self'? I had no answers.

These questions led me to write in my notes:

If an individual's body physics and chemistry is constantly changing and if the mind looks at things or thinks about things that are in a constant state of flux, then is it not doubtful that 'I' exists as a durable and constant identity? But I cannot formulate any concrete thoughts on these propositions and I am staggered by their implications. There is, I believe, implicit in this thinking another way of seeing the world.

I was constantly being reminded by lectures and books that the Buddha taught that suffering could be eliminated by practising meditation, by developing the mind to gain wisdom in the nature of greed, hatred, and ignorance and thereby eliminating them. By meditating one can see truth for one's self – truth which supposedly lies within everyone.

This thinking seemed paradoxical to me. If the Buddha taught that there should be no attachment to anything, including the Buddha and one's self, how could man turn inward, into himself, to discover the great truths, when he was supposedly trying to eliminate attachment to the 'self'.

I was both intrigued and confused. How was meditation going to allow me – a human being with five ordinary senses – to look inside myself to find the truth?

According to most Buddhists, answers cannot be found by intellectual puzzling or scholarship, but through meditation – the only means through which man can obtain true wisdom.

I was even more confused about meditation when the scholar at Wat Sraket made it clear that the only way to eliminate the causes of suffering, particularly greed, which he felt was the primary cause of suffering, was to practise vipassana, or insight meditation. To date, I had only been practising and learning about samadhi meditation. This was my first knowledge that there were differing points of view on the value of the various meditational methods taught by Theravada Buddhists.

My mentor explained that samadhi meditation, while a method of mind development, could only bring tranquillity through its technique of developing concentration or one-pointedness of the mind. It could not bring wisdom into the nature of reality. Vipassana developed insight – insight into truth, into the true states of nature. The practice of vipassana could give humans 'panna', or wisdom, which was, in turn, part of the path which led to nibbana.

It troubled me little at that time or later on that one meditational method supposedly had more far-reaching effects than the other. Both methods or techniques seemed to be concerned with the development of the potential of the mind. I was far more concerned about how we, through meditation, could extinguish such seemingly common and consuming human character traits as avarice, hate, and delusion. It seemed impossible, but I struggled on, trying to be open to all stimuli, all thoughts, all experiences. Then one night during meditation at Wat Bovornives, I had an unusual and totally unexpected experience.

## Chapter Four

> People have worldly passions which lead them into
> delusions and suffering.
> *The Teaching of Buddha*, Bukkyo Dendo Kyoka

TONIGHT, as I entered the friendly upstairs meditating room in the Abbot's guti, I was aware of the mingling of jasmine and incense with the musky tropical air – a familiar smell which I had grown to like.

As usual it was dark except for the customary candles hopscotching up the tiered shelves of the altar to light the images of the Buddha. Surrounded by flowers, small images rested on the lower altar shelves as if in attendance on the large tranquil Buddha image which was seated at the top. Flickering candle flames gently cast lingering shadows; the overhead fan tossed and tumbled perfumed air.

The saffron-robed Abbot sat Buddha-like before the altar. In the candlelight, his brown skin and saffron robe seemed to merge and crystallize, transforming him into a gilt and bronze statue.

As I watched the Abbot, sitting in a mist of incense, I thought again and again about his simple meditation instruction for tonight's session. 'Be mindful of your meditation subject.' Usually the instruction was to be mindful of breathing, but this seemed to be different. I puzzled at its meaning; it seemed so vague.

As I sat there considering the various things his instruction might mean, I thought about the monk Buddhadasa, who wrote about the feasibility of meditating on subjects which could be determined from character traits that a particular meditator might possess. Maybe it was something like this that the Abbot was referring to.

I recalled Buddhadasa's writings about the character types or classes of temperaments. I had contemplated the various types and recorded them in my notebook: lustful, hateful, dull, faithful (blind faith), intelligent, and speculative.

Buddhadasa believed that the meditator, before undertaking

serious meditation, must understand his own nature and mode of interaction with his environment. Over the past days, I had thought about his analysis of people and decided that lustful, I was not; dull, not really; faithful, not at all; speculative, probably not; intelligent, maybe; but hateful, I was for certain. He cautioned meditators to be careful of their own self-evaluations for delusion would certainly be involved. I agreed, but I knew that I possessed the ability to hate. I could hate to the extent that it could give me a thundering headache and cause constrictions in my throat that were most alarming.

In my notebook, I had copied his description of the hating character type and what this type might do to eliminate this trait.

The Hating Character-type: This is the person who easily becomes angry, who is short-tempered and liable to become irritated without reason. The environment recommended for this type is just the reverse of the one beneficial to the Lustful type. It is recommended that the person of hating character-type should create, or live in, an environment where everything is tidy, orderly, beautiful and pleasing to the eye. His dwelling should be perfectly neat and clean, spick and span, free from anything irritating. His clothing should be of fine quality, of pleasing colour, not smelly and of smooth, superior material. If a 'bhikkhu' he should go for alms to a village that is very clean and tidy and where the people are cultured and well-mannered. The environment he lives in should be in no way depressing but suitably clean, orderly, and tidy. He should spend more time sitting and lying down then standing and walking. Other minor things should be arranged along the lines indicated. As to colour, he should give preference to dark green, the least stimulating of all colours.*

Sitting in the fragrant quiet, I decided that someday I should try to meditate on hatred, but for now I did not know how. Sometime, when it seemed appropriate, I decided that I should ask how one went about such a meditation task. Now I wanted

* Buddhadasa, *Anapanasati*, p. 29

to meditate and since I only knew how to do mindfulness of breathing meditation, I began breathing-in and breathing-out.

As I became more and more aware of my breathing, as usual, my mind, or an energy force or mass, seemed to form somewhere out in front of my nose. Then the flickering shades of blue filled infinity. Beautiful blues, psychedelic, churning and spinning in a multitude of hues from purple to light aqua. The flickering became less erratic and in the midst of the blue, far, far away there was a light tan pinpoint – a tiny hole in infinity. As I continued my breathing, the pinprick grew larger and larger, always retaining a somewhat round shape.

Eventually the tan shape, which was no longer a hole but the opposite of a hole – a circle that existed independently – began to pulsate like a heart. Then it began to pulsate with my heart. With each beat, it slowly grew larger. A phosphorous glow, almost halo-like, became evident and flashed brightly with pulsating rhythm.

The tan, and now a bit grey, circle was no longer just a circle; it was a heart. As it grew larger, the luminous follicles that surrounded it grew brighter with each beat.

With my awareness pulling toward the glowing, beating heart, it exploded into a sunburst of colours. Remembering that I should ignore images and colours, I returned to fuller concentration on my breathing, taking long breaths. Eventually the repeating explosions of glistening baubles dwindled and dripped downward from their heights to form a shape – a shape that became the arteries of a heart. The cascading colours disappeared; the brilliant blues became browns.

A brown hole appeared, much like the original pinprick in infinity, but this time it was darker and bigger. It grew and eventually became the inside of a heart. The heart was open – the top one quarter was cut away to expose the inside. In the centre of this greyish-brown heart, there was a brown hole choked with dark, slimy sludge. This heart was trying to beat, but nothing could move. The hole seemed unable to bear the strain of the sludge, pressing against its sides. It appeared that if the muddy sludge inside could not escape, then the heart would be destroyed. The clogged heart twisted and strained in spasms resembling contractions in childbirth.

The contortions crescendoed. With a great gush, the brackish sediment burst forth from the hole and spilled over an immense area. The sludge continued to flow into the infinite distance until the hole, now free from the corroding slush, became a normal heart ventricle and began to beat again as a normal heart might beat. It seemed to beat with my heart, yet it was a heart distinctly different from mine. I couldn't tell if it were my heart or not, but it was a human heart. I felt no emotion nor attachment to the heart, although I was much interested in it. At the same time, I was aware of breathing-in and breathing out.

At some point, the pulsating heart became blue and whole again. Then, softly, it merged with the melange of vivid blue and purple colours that twirled about in ever-decreasing concentric circles around a tiny pin prick of light in infinity.

Mysteriously and seemingly uncontrollably, meditation ends. This night, I particularly wanted to cling to the blue, soothing colours. I tried to hold fast to the breathing, but it couldn't be forced and eventually and slowly I opened my eyes. The Abbott was gone. Two lay meditators still sat on the little saffron rugs in the dim candlelight. I did not want to move. I seemed to be free. As I sat there quietly, I became aware of a floating sensation, a complete release from everything. The feeling was fragile and yet pervasive – yet a new feeling. I reflected on the evening. My mind drifted to my pre-empted desire to meditate on hatred; to the usual meditation on mindfulness of breathing; and to this continuing sense of freedom.

Then I superficially thought of the man whose very name could stir a sense of hate in me, but there was no response, no feeling of hatred. I thought of him again a little longer and still no response. I thought of him again still longer and of some of the evil ways in which he had used me and other innocent people for his own aggrandizement. But it evoked no emotion! None!

Only when I was outside the guti putting on my sandals did I realize how weak and tired I was – as if I had experienced a great catharsis.

Slowly and mindfully, I walked through the darkened compound of Wat Bovornives. Temple bells tinkled ever so lightly in the night breezes. A few Pali chants, coming from the quarters of older monks, softly met the slight wind. Essentially the wat was dark, at least below. Above, the moon touched the delicate glasswork on the tiers of up-turned roofs which were stretching upward as if in jubilation.

I stopped to admire the moon's art.

In the distance I could see what seemed to be another moon giving shape and ethereal colours to the Golden Mountain at Wat Sraket. The moon's discriminating light embellished these lofty religious edifices, projecting mystery and art into the night.

Observing this shadowy art, I recalled one of the teachings of Buddha.

Suffering is caused by desires, by liking or not liking. Eliminate the desires, the defilements of the mind, at their roots and suffering will cease.

I thought again of the man who normally could arouse such unhealthy emotions in me, but now I felt no hate toward him. There was only a neutral feeling. Had I just demonstrated what my Buddhist teachers had been saying – that hate is a source of much suffering and that it could be eliminated through meditation?

How long lasting would this absence of hatred be? Could I carry this neutral feeling all the way back to my room? Had I, indeed, meditated on hatred even though I had not thought I would be able to do so?

I was tired. The walk home seemed long, but my weariness

seemed compensated for by the sensation of being free – free of what I did not know, but free.

As usual after meditation, I did not want anything to eat and this night I did not want anything to drink either. I wrote in my notebook of my experience and went to bed, serene in this new found sense of freedom which I could not understand.

## Chapter Five

> ... it is certain that the purely physical fear of death,
> that horror and utter revulsion that seizes the
> majority of us at the idea of death, is absent from
> most Orientals.
>
> H. Fielding Hall, *The Soul of a People*

THE world was dawn-grey as my taxi sped through the back streets and lanes of Bangkok. I was heading for the airport and eventually to a town in northern Thailand.

As the taxi hurried away from the old sections of Bangkok along the Chao Phraya River – away from an area which had been my home for the past weeks – I glanced back to see the silhouette of the Golden Mountain chedi of Wat Sraket bold and strong against the dawning day. As I watched the silhouette disappear from sight, I thought of my experiences studying meditation at Wat Bovornives, learning about Buddhist philosophy at Wat Sraket, and the many dialogues with Buddhist friends. Although I had experienced disappointments, and sometimes fear, it had been a beautiful experience – mystifying, joyful, and contemplative.

I was aware that I had taken just the tiniest of steps into the world of Theravada Buddhism and meditation. I wanted to know more, yet concepts that had seemed uncomplicated when reading about them in Connecticut were no longer simple as I struggled to *know* them within myself.

Some things that troubled me earlier no longer were bothersome. I had gradually become familiar with the detached behaviour of monks. I now understood why the Abbot, on our initial meeting, did not acknowledge in any way my gift of flowers. I wasn't giving the flowers to *him*, but to the *wat*, for monks cannot possess anything and, more importantly, I was making merit for myself by giving. I had also become accustomed to wai-ing and thanking monks and in return only receiving a passive non-look. But becoming accustomed to the actualization of detachment in others was far different from knowing detachment within myself.

I didn't know how to be detached – I wanted, liked, disliked, yearned, and desired. I came to the conclusion that, in truth, I possessed all the traits that led one to a life of attachment and consequently to suffering.

Thinking about my yearnings and wantings, I recalled most vividly the day at Wat Sraket when my teacher had pointed out that monks don't paint, write great novels, compose music, or create movie extravaganzas because these are forms of cravings or wantings. It was difficult for me to understand that writing a book was a craving, particularly when being creative was a coveted trait in Western society. I tried to argue with him, but no matter how philanthropic I made my own purposes for writing, the ultimate purpose always resulted in me *wanting* something – even though it was just the wanting for people to read my books so *they* might learn about another part of the world for their own benefit.

I often reflected on our conversation of that day. I still did not understand. I could, however, agree that the process of creativity often involves suffering. This I knew from personal experience.

I continued to wonder if I, an American, who had grown up in an environment and among institutions which criticized

detachment, stressed involvement, and lauded creativity, could ever have any chance of understanding detachment which seemed critically important in Buddhism and a goal of meditation. I mused that perhaps it is irrevocably true that East is East and West is West and never the two shall meet.

It was confusing to think about these things, so I dismissed them to think about Chiang Mai, the town in northern Thailand where there was a meditating wat with living facilities for females that might accept foreign women. In Bangkok, even though I had spent a considerable part of my time in the wat, I knew little about wat life. I had remained the outsider who came to the wat for a few hours, then departed. I was hoping that in Chiang Mai I would have the opportunity to live in a religious compound. Perhaps I would even be fortunate enough to become part of the wat life; maybe I would no longer be the outsider.

The cool morning air whipping through the open taxi windows, carrying with it a heavy scent from the jasmine lei that dangled from the driver's rear-view mirror, helped calm my worrying mind. On the outskirts of Bangkok, the taxi swung onto a small lane paralleled by a klong laden with gigantic lotus. The sun, only inches above the horizon, had already touched the klong, pushing strength into the unfolding blossoms. Soft pink and snowy white, the lotus blossoms, resembling a mosaic so often repeated in temple motifs, covered the waterway as if it were a flowered drapery put there by an ancient artist.

This klong, one of the last clean and beautiful canals remaining in Bangkok, stretched for several miles along the roadway. In one area, several men, waist deep in the waters, were collecting the large unopened lotus buds which would be bought in markets by the faithful to be given as offerings to monks or placed before Buddha images in neighbourhood wats.

Whether caused by the cool, jasmine-scented air, or by the sight of the brown-skinned men gathering one of nature's most exquisite flowers, or by the pure excitement of anticipation, I impulsively wanted to keep this morning. I asked the driver if he would drive as slow as possible along the klong. I wanted to enjoy the birth of this new day so artistically accompanied by man and nature.

Too soon, the taxi left the quiet lane and drove to the big four-lane superhighway. Another twenty minutes and we would be at the airport.

Being the first passenger to check-in with Thai Airways, I sat alone in the open-air waiting room writing in my diary for some time. Then the quietness of early morning was displaced by a growing crowd of passengers and friends.

My diary-writing was completely disrupted by a mumbling wave of voices moving my way. First came an older monk, followed close behind by a young novice of about fourteen. Behind those in saffron came a dozen Thai people: women dressed in black and several men dressed in white with black arm bands, designated a funeral party. They sat on the couches next to mine and from their conversations I learned that the older monk had been flown up from southern Thailand to attend the cremation ceremonies of a member of his family. Now he was returning with the novice who was his attendant. Since the older monk had a novice attending him, it probably meant that the monk had been in the monkhood for a long time, or perhaps he was an Abbot of a southern monastery.

As I watched the two monks holding their boarding passes, I tried to remember if I had ever seen monks flying before. Since monks do not drive, they either travel by bus, taxi, or are chauffeured around by a merit-making Buddhist. As I thought about the monkhood rule that a monk could not touch a woman, I wondered if the chances for a touching incident were greater in a small, compact airplane or in a jammed bus. On buses, the monks either sit on the wide seat in the back or in the front seat with the driver. I wondered where monks sit on airplanes.

Listening to these people, who wore the clothes of mourning, I heard no maudlin words. As they talked happily of travelling, their children, and the in-process modernization of Bangkok International Airport, I recognized a feeling or an attitude that I had known many times before when attending cremation ceremonies at a wat or visiting the homes of the deceased.

This feeling that I often sensed among the Buddhist mourners almost defied definition. Death to them seems to exact no pity, no rebellion, no mournful wailings; nor does it promote exultations or rejoicings. Death brings with it a mood, fragile and tender.

The mourners reveal these qualities, yet death somehow does not command the importance, the finality, that it does to Westerners.

As I listened to the gentle chatter next to me, I began to think about the general differences between the Eastern and Western concepts of death, and I wrote in my notebook:

It's not true that Southeast Asians consider life valueless. To those Westerners who say that life 'is cheap' and doesn't matter to Orientals, I say that they have neglected to understand a basic Buddhist belief.

The Oriental views himself and his world differently. He views death and dying with less pure physical fear because he believes that there are many more lives to live.

Perhaps the fear for the Theravada Buddhist is that he might be unfortunate enough to suffer a violent and untimely death. According to local beliefs, death caused by violence such as in war, childbirth, or in an accident can leave the 'soul' tormented and wandering, unable, for some reason, to be reborn soon.

Maybe it is this fear of an untimely death that prompts many Thais to wear necklaces of good-luck charms which supposedly are blessed by someone, often a monk, who reportedly possesses extraordinary powers.

After observing both young American and Thai and Lao soldiers under the duress of battle, I have often wondered if the Buddhist soldier's greatest fear was not of being killed, but of killing another and having to suffer tremendously in this life or another for his heinous deed.

For many Westerners, death is horror. Yet it is the Western religious creeds which dwell on death and instruct the followers on how to avoid the fear of death. Religious people and death-bed rites are available to aid the dying to accept death, yet death remains, for many, a trauma of the gravest dimensions.

Buddhist teachings focus on life – since life and death are one. Death (or changing) is only a part of life. Of course, there are rites and rituals attached to the cremation or burial of a Buddhist and the families reflect sadness. But because the Theravada Buddhist believes that he has many lives to live – hundreds, perhaps hundreds of thousands, yet to come – there is an absence of finality in the cessation of one. For the Buddhist, death is not a trauma, but more the continuation of a constant process of changing, decaying, and arising that somehow lies outside the notion of death as a finality.

The essence of this understanding of death is softly chanted by monks at funerals – 'All things in "samsara" (the world of birth and death) are impermanent. To be happy there can be no clinging.'

Eventually the Chiang Mai flight was called, and minutes later we were airborne for an approximated two-hour flight to the highlands of northern Thailand. My eyes followed the Chao Phraya River (which in Thai means Noble Lord) as it carved a coiled and muddy swathe through fields flat, brown, and cracked from lack of rain. The monsoons would soon fill the cracks; the Chao Phraya would overflow its banks, sending waters over the brown fields, and in weeks the seeming infertile land would be lush and green with tender rice shoots.

When the rejuvenating monsoon rains come, flooding fields, road, and villages, the monks, almost paradoxically, retreat to the confines of their wats. Historically, it was considered a dangerous time for monks to be travelling about the countryside. During the rainy season, there was the threat of malaria. The Thais say it is better for the monks not to be trampling tender rice shoots and not to be venturing into waters that contain many living creatures, including fish which can be caught in rice paddies during the rainy season. A travelling monk could accidentally kill some living creature – a prohibited act. In present times, monks venture out during the rainy season but usually only with permission, and the monastery rules stipulate that normally they must return to their home wat before dark. At this time of year, it is expected that all monks will be cloistered within the wats for intensive study of Buddhist scriptures and meditation practices.

But since there were still a few weeks until the monsoons, visibility remained good. So I decided that I would try to follow the twisting Chao Phraya River to the old capital of Ayutthaya, the Siamese capital for over four hundred years. It was at Ayutthaya that some of the fiercest and most important battles in Thai history took place.

There were so few uninhabited areas remaining that I wondered if I could find the old ruins amidst the many villages and wats that lined the river's banks. Small teakwood houses, nondescript against barren fields of almost the same colour, monotonously cluttered the countryside. Unlike the brown houses of the farmers, the religious compounds scattered profusely over the land were miniature citadels of colour and glitter.

The temple buildings, sun-drenched in yellows, whites, and saffrons and a-twinkle with blue and green mosaic glasswork, expressed the devotion of a people to their religion in the form of temple building which is considered to be one of the best forms of merit-making. Again today I wondered how it was possible financially for the Thai people to build and support so many wats.

I had begun to count the wats when I saw Ayutthaya – large patches of crumbling bricks and giant columns jutting up like markers of ancient space travellers. Abandoned, the city now lay silent, a majestic ruin among rice paddies. These ruins were constant reminders to the Thais of their neighbours to the West, the Burmese, who, during the 18th century had not only destroyed their glorious capital and shattered the kingdom of Ayutthaya, but had burned their historic and religious writings and desecrated their religious art.

I tried to visualize the Burmese armies advancing toward Ayutthaya in 1767 – moving across low mountains, through tropical undergrowth and open rice fields with a pageantry of spear-carrying soldiers in full regalia, of mahouts and giant war elephants – in 1767 to lay siege to an imperial city of over a million people.

As I looked at the wide, lazy river, so nobly named, I thought of the suffering that the Thai people had endured along its banks. In particular I remembered that less than one hundred years ago near Ayutthaya on the Chao Phraya a royal tragedy occurred that still evokes sympathy from the Thais, and was perhaps the reason for subsequent changes in the rules of court etiquette.

As recently as one hundred years ago, the King of Thailand was so sacred that commoners were not allowed to lay their eyes on him. When he travelled about the country, his subjects were asked to close their shutters, thus reducing the chances of an accidental glance which could result in severe punishment. When approaching the King, the subject had to prostrate himself by crawling towards him on his stomach.

In 1881 when these strict rules and protocols applied not only to the King but to his whole court, lovely Suanda, a Queen in Chulalongkorn's court, was travelling down the Chao Phraya when her royal barge overturned. The Queen, heavily pregnant, floundered helplessly in the murky waters. While her attendants looked on, she drowned. No one in her entourage dared touch her; it was forbidden on penalty of death.

Today Thai people are no longer forbidden a glance at their King and Queen, yet most bow their heads and kneel when they pass by. Thai commoners are no longer required to prostrate themselves before the King, yet most do. To most of the people in Thailand, King Bhumibol Adulyadej, King Rama IX, is a revered and loved being.

As I thought about the attitude of the common people of Thailand, Laos, and Cambodia toward their kings, or in the case of the Cambodians, towards Prince Sihanouk, I knew that reverence for their king was still very much alive, and a consistent manifestation of their belief in rebirth and kamma

– a belief which gave them hope that in the future, in some life, they too, might have a kamma befitting royalty.

Thinking about the political ramifications of this reverence, I unconsciously began looking to the east toward Cambodia, the home of the Great Khmer civilization which fostered this cult.

As the plane began its descent for Chiang Mai, it dropped first into the Lampang Valley, lush with green vegetable gardens and lacy lumyai orchards – a valley rich in Siamese history. It was here in these mountains and valleys, during the 13th to 16th centuries, that an independent kingdom of Thai people established significant control over virtually all of northern Thailand, into the Shan States of Burma, and even into Laos. This kingdom was called Lan Na Thai, the Kingdom of a Million Rice Fields. Then in the 16th century, Burmese armies marched against and captured Chiang Mai, the walled and moated capital city. For the next 300 years there was intermittent warfare. The architecture, artisan crafts and cuisine brought in by the Burmese overlords still flourishes in the Chiang Mai area.

For most of the people in northern Thailand, including the ethnic Thai and the hilltribe minorities, Bangkok, the present capital, is not only remote – some five hundred miles away – but it seems another world in climate, language, and modernization. The native inhabitants of northern Thailand speak 'Kam Muang', a dialect more akin to the Shan language spoken by the Thais who inhabit the Shan States of northeast Burma. The people of the north are often embarrassed by their inability to speak Bangkok Thai.

My self-designed history lesson was about to end; the 'Fasten Seat Belt' sign came on. I complied and nestled down to relax. What lay ahead for me? Would the Abbot at Wat Muang Mang grant permission for me to stay in his wat? I had heard that only intensive meditation was taught there, and I didn't know what was involved in such a discipline. What would I have to do?

I thought about my Thai friend's warning. 'Be very careful.

In intensive meditation you can go crazy. You can go too far and then you can't come back. Be careful!' Similar warnings had been issued by other Thai friends and even by some monks. I had heard about the young American man who became a monk in Thailand and at some point in his meditation study thought he saw a moon that beckoned him to follow. He followed the moon and walked out of a second-storey window.

I had heard other rumours of meditators, mostly foreigners, committing violent acts, becoming alarmingly depressed, psychotic, or manifesting other mental aberrations.

These bizarre happenings interested me, and just days before I left Bangkok, I had the opportunity to ask a psychiatrist, a Westerner who had been a monk himself, if there were dangers in meditation. He assured me that from his professional experience, foreign meditators who went crazy – as the Thais say – either had histories of mental disturbances in their own or family backgrounds or suffered from debilitating physical causes, such as malaria, which helped set off unusual and sometimes desperate reactions.

I didn't think that I had any repressed psychological problems that intensive meditation might bring to the surface, but, as my Buddhist teachers repeatedly reminded me, it is very difficult to judge one's self because delusion is always around to confuse.

I had felt for some time, and my psychiatrist acquaintance had confirmed my beliefs, that for best results when dealing with advanced meditation a competent meditation instructor is an absolute necessity. It seemed to me a foolish venture to try to teach oneself to meditate beyond a certain point. Later, I came to believe that in intensive meditation not only is having a competent instructor nearby all the time a necessity, but the instructor must also be someone whom the meditator trusts and respects.

But for now as the plane slipped down on the short runway, I noticed an excessive amount of perspiration on my palms. It was not from the excitement of flying, but from the unnerving anticipation of what lay ahead of me.

As the plane taxied to the small terminal and as heat quickly filled the cabin, I studied the words that I had written in my notebook :

KAMMA – Is it possible? Is it the unfolding of my kamma that has brought me here, half-way around the world to seek to understand Buddhism?
INTENSIVE MEDITATION – Voyage into the unknown. Where can it take me? Through death, to madness, or perhaps to taste of tranquillity?

## Chapter Six

If you have the opportunity to practise the Insight
meditation, even just for a few days or seven days,
it would be to your advantage to do so.

Upasika Naeb Mahairandonda
*Development of Insight*

SHE fumbled with the keys trying to find one to unlock the
door to room number four. She was a mae-chee, dressed in white
with a shaved head. She looked much like the little mae-chee
at Wat Sraket, but this woman was bigger and didn't smile.

She opened the door for me and disappeared. Slowly I
entered the dark, hot room. The Abbot of Wat Muang Mang
had given me permission to stay only if I promised to become
a student of vipassana meditation, the meditation technique
taught in his wat. After receiving permission, I had taken time
to assemble a few living essentials and now I stood in a very
small room – my room in an intensive meditating wat in
northern Thailand.

Institutional pea-green paint was marred with marks of long
usage. From the high ceiling dangled one long cord which
ended in a bare light-bulb. The furnishings were few: one
board-slab bed with a thin straw mat on it; one very low,
small table, apparently hand-hewn some years ago; and one
ancient, rusting folding chair.

Two shuttered windows tightly closed were trimmed with
once-white nylon curtains, thin, worn, and dusty, which hung
across screens darkened with grime and dirt. Two small brown
vases held the remains of flowers, brown and dead except for
one salmon coloured rose. Beside the vase was a tin mug
jammed with partially burned incense sticks, a package of
tooth-picks, and a small box of matches.

In the corner near the door was a grass broom, a tin bucket
filled with dirty rags, and a spitoon gaily decorated with
festive flowers. A bit of old sheet hanging from the screened
door fluttered occasionally in the lazy afternoon breeze.

Next I explored the small enclosure opposite the bed. It was the 'bathroom'. It contained a large brown water jar, a small lavatory, and a Thai-style toilet which one uses by squatting down over a hole in the floor and then flushes by panning water into it. I tried the water-tap at the lavatory; it didn't work. As I stood in the dimness, I saw several cockroaches scramble down the toilet and I became aware of a distinctively strong odour.

The room was stifling hot and I perspired profusely as I began arranging my few belongings: towels, soap, candles, a cup, bug spray, flash-light, air mattress, two sheets for the cool hours of morning, books on Buddhism, a bunch of bananas, and a thermos of boiled water. In most wats the drinking water is kept in huge, open earthern vats resembling rain barrels. The water in this wat was probably safe to drink, but I couldn't be certain. I felt that studying vipassana would be an all-consuming task and one thing I did not need was a bout of dysentery.

With my belongings in order, I looked around the room and remembered the monk's description of the living accomodations that a hateful type of person, like myself, must have to be able to meditate – clean, attractive, and free from any irritations or annoyances. For a panicked moment, I felt that it would be impossible to live in this room. My doubts subsided when I focused my attention on the fact that after years of striving to live in a Buddhist wat, I now stood in my own cell in a meditating wat where I soon was to become a student of vipassana meditation.

A bit annoyed at myself for being so concerned for the 'I', I went outside to open the heavy wooden shutters. As I was latching them open, I heard a slow shuffling sound. I turned to see an old woman, severely hunch-backed, coming toward me on a common porch.

She asked me in Thai how I was. I answered fine and asked her the same question. She was fine, too. Whereupon we just looked at each other. She began moving closer to me until she was very near. She was inspecting me at close range; she undoubtedly had bad eyesight. After some minutes of scrutinizing me, she shuffled to the edge of the porch to spit out a long rivulet of red betel-nut juice that we both watched coagulate into a dark red puddle in the sand. After she spat, she returned to study me further. Finally she asked if I had come to study vipassana. When I answered that I had, her lips, reddened by the betel-nut juice, parted in a warm smile that indicated friendship and revealed black teeth, darkened by years of betel-nut chewing.

I felt uncomfortable just standing by my window, so I sat down on the porch edge. She followed me and continued to stand over me for some time murmuring repeatedly, 'Very hot, isn't it?' To which I agreed each time. After some time, she abruptly turned and shuffled away to disappear into room number one.

I returned to my room and folded the sheets into a pillow so that I could have a cushion to sit on while resting on the board bed. I decided if I sat very still I might feel cooler.

No sooner had I gotten comfortable than I felt someone observing me. I cautiously looked toward the windows to find a face peeping in at me. I said hello in Thai and the face smiled and moved away. Only minutes later, another face appeared at the dark screens. I repeated a hello and the face, like the other one, disappeared. This time I moved close to the window to try to see who it was. I caught a glimpse of someone in white clothes with a shaved head walking away slowly.

Of course! The mae-chee, my neighbours, were coming to take a look at the farang woman living in their quarters.

The crippled old lady had reported the news well. Soon several other faces appeared mysteriously at my window, including a couple of small children who took turns lifting each other up so they could see the farang.

I smiled and put my head against the wall to rest. I was tired, very tired. I supposed that it was only natural reaction to my new environment with so many unknowns awaiting me. As I sat in the extreme heat, a tenseness began welling up inside me as I began to think about the days ahead. Here I was in a wat to practise vipassana meditation, something about which I knew nothing. I barely recognized the word. The scholar at Wat Sraket had used it when explaining that the practice of vipassana was the only route to nibbana – the only route to wisdom.

My life would be quite different here. No longer would I be visiting or studying in a wat for several hours a day, then leaving and going back to familiar surroundings. I began to feel that same haunting fear that I had known so well during my first days at Wat Bovornives.

Undoubtedly I would be expected to fit into the routine common to this wat. But what was that routine? How did I get food? Could I walk around the wat freely or were parts of it, where the monks lived, off limits to women? Could a woman go into all buildings or were some open to men only? I did not know the answers and I did not know whom I should ask?

Disturbed by these unanswerable questions, I considered practising mindfulness of breathing to calm myself, but felt that it would be a losing battle. So I just remained sitting on the bed staring at some Thai writing on the wall while trying to ignore the sultry heat. Then I thought about my first meeting with the Abbot which had occurred the day before.

As I approached the Abbot's guti, I saw him sitting in a

half-lotus position on a raised platform in the outer room of his modest two-room shelter, reading Buddhist scriptures from a narrow red book made from palm leaves. He was a particularly stout man, unusual for a Thai, about fifty years old. I noticed that he was bald except for a shadowy growth of black hair that outlined the sides of his head in Friar Tuck fashion. I recorded this bit of information; it would be a way to distinguish the Abbot from the other monks. Since all monks, no matter what their rank or seniority in a monastery, shave their heads and eyebrows twice a month, wear the saffron robes in identical ways, and even walk in a similar fashion as directed by the rules of the monkhood, it was often difficult for me to distinguish one from another.

Luckily for me, there was a bespectacled novice in his early twenties, who spoke English and happened to be visiting this wat for a few days, who could act as an interpreter for me. The Abbot spoke no English and although I could speak some Thai, I certainly did not speak it well enough to discuss anything philosophical. Nor was I comfortable speaking it to an exalted person such as an Abbot for fear of using the wrong tonal sound for some words, and thus saying something embarrassing.

I recalled that after the novice introduced me, the Abbot remained quiet, looking at me in almost the same fashion as had the Abbot of Wat Bovornives, though he seemed less detached. I thought of my dress, which was probably too short because I could see one of my knees showing as I knelt. I was embarrassed. His eyes, brown and soft, studied my face and hands which I was holding in respect.

Now as I thought about that brief meeting, I had a good feeling about the Abbot who seemed gentle, compassionate, and very alert. I hoped that I was correct in my evaluation.

Eventually darkness came, bringing with it a soft breeze which intermittently created a tinkling from temple bells. In the soft air the cooings of birds making last minute adjustments in their roosts of dark leaves seemed to harmonize with the hushed voices of monks and novices as they, too, settled in for the night.

It wasn't wise to turn on my lights because if I did I knew that hordes of mosquitoes would invade, so I sat on my bed surrounded by a darkness made docile by nature's sounds of early night.

This tranquillity was interrupted by a man's voice outside my door, calling my name. I turned on the light and went to the door to find the Abbot and the novice standing there. The Abbot quietly asked if he could see if my room was all right. As I told him that it was fine, he pushed open the door to look for himself, but didn't enter – this being a woman's room.

He looked about and seemed pleased. He stepped back from the door, then hesitated and spoke in a hushed voice to the novice. The novice looked at me shyly before speaking. 'The Abbot wants to know if you will keep the eight precepts while you are in this wat?'

I quickly tried to remember all eight of them, but couldn't. Hesitatingly, I told the waiting Abbot that I would *try* to observe the eight precepts. What else could I say? He smiled ever so slightly and walked away.

I closed the screen door, turned off the light, and sat down on my bed . . . the eight precepts! What were they? With my flash-light, I dug into my suitcase to find a book which might list them and by flash-light I read:

EIGHT PRECEPTS

I undertake the steps of training
1) To refrain from killing, which includes anything alive such as a mosquito, fly, or red ant.
2) To refrain from taking what is not given.
3) To refrain from sexual activity.
4) To refrain from false speech which includes not only lying but harsh speech, back-biting, and idle gossip.
5) To refrain from fermented and distilled liquors and from drugs which confuse the mind.
6) To refrain from taking food after noon until dawn of the next day.

7) To refrain from seeing shows, attending dances, or becoming involved in any kind of entertainment.
8) To refrain from sleeping on a soft and luxurious bed.

As I contemplated the list of precepts, I wondered if there were any possible way that I could adhere to all of these encompassing rules. If I could not, would he ask me to leave?

There would be no difficulty in refraining from sexual relations, or drinking liquors, or taking drugs. I had no intention of becoming involved in any kind of entertainment. I wondered if light conversation might be considered a form of entertainment?

I wasn't too certain that I understood the precept forbiddening one to take what is not given. I wondered if it included more than the obvious act of stealing. To refrain from harsh speech didn't seem too difficult. I was among strangers; I wouldn't have much to talk about. I thought I could dispense with the air mattress to sleep on the plank bed and it was undoubtedly possible to exist on two meals a day, both before noon.

But I wasn't certain how to handle the 'no killing' precept. Tropical lands are infested with bugs, spiders, cockroaches, and hordes of other little creatures that plague humans. While most of them are troublesome, they are, at least to me, tolerable, except for the mosquito who, with his blood-sucking livelihood, could certainly cause me discomfort. Since this precept prohibited the killing of any living creature, I would have to learn to use tremendous restraint and gently brush away any mosquito or ant rather than slap it to death. What would I do about all the cockroaches that lived in the toilet?

I lay down on the board bed to think. It was certainly neither a soft nor a luxurious bed; it was extremely hard and at the moment uncomfortable.

I was restless. The room was hot; my mind fatigued. First I contemplated the eight precepts, then I began to wonder, perhaps for the hundredth time, what the real difference between samadhi and vipassana meditation could be. I was confused. I knew that if I really wanted to know then I must practise vipassana myself. I could still hear the Abbot at Wat Bovornives telling me: 'One's self is the big book'.

Perhaps tomorrow I would know something of vipassana, but now on my first night at Wat Muang Mang, alone in the shadowy darkness of my cell, trying to gather the courage to begin a journey into intensive meditation, I felt hollow, lonely, and hungry, and most of all I was apprehensive – apprehensive about what might happen to me in this journey to eliminate the self.

## Chapter Seven

Do not forget that we pay homage to the Buddha
because he has shown us the method of mental
development for the attainment of nibbana; namely
the application of mindfulness which all other
teachers in the world could not teach.

Mahairandonda
*Development of Insight*

I was awakened by a resonant ringing of a gong, accompanied
by a cacophonous howling chorus of temple dogs. They howled
as if they were being tortured. Even after the third and last
ringing of the gong had ceased, the dogs hung on to their
mournful and unearthly cries. I looked at my watch; it was
4:00 am.

I sat up and looked out the window. In a short time, monks
moved from the darkness of their guti into a candle-lit
building to chant. The mellow chanting lullingly filled the
previously silent courtyard.

Unsuccessfully, I tried to sleep. I closed my eyes and rested,
maybe even dozed, until the shrieking and grinding of metal
on metal brought me to the window again. A samlor (a three-
wheeled pedalled ricksha) driver was braking his poorly
equipped vehicle to a halt near the monks' quarters. He dis-
mounted and gingerly carried a package into the shadows of
the guti. Either he had a friend or relative in this wat to whom
he was bringing a gift, or someone had hired him to deliver
an offering.

As I watched for the samlor driver to return, I noticed
monks and novices, their black alms bowls partially hidden by
their flowing saffron robes, floating silently through the temple
gates, one by one. With their eyes downcast, their gait precise
and slow, each foot being mindfully placed a certain distance
ahead of the other, they moved into the fragility of dawn to
walk the lanes and streets affording the faithful the opportunity to make merit by giving them food for their morning and pre-noon meals.

After a few monks had passed through the gate, I went

outside to see if there was enough light to see the lines in the palm of my hand. It seemed too dark to be able to do this. It is said that a monk cannot leave his wat for morning alming rounds until he can clearly see these lines. Sure enough, these lines were visible.

Sitting on the veranda, I watched a number of monks, including the Abbot, and novices disappear through the gate. When it seemed that all the monks had left the wat, I walked to the entrance gates.

A little, common meandering lane passed by the wat. Fragrant flowers in hues of purple, red, pink, orange, and white adorned the small two-storeyed teakwood houses, giving a contented artistry to the box-like buildings on stilts.

It was odd that during my many trips to Chiang Mai, I had never seen or heard of Wat Muang Mang. It did not appear on the tourist maps as did other more prestigious or ancient wats.

As I lingered by the gate, the household opposite the gates began stirring. An old Thai man descended from the upstairs

sleeping area to open the large wooden doors that revealed a small dressmaking shop on the ground level. Next he gathered up several red clay water jars from a small wooden shelter that stood near the lane and busied himself filling them with fresh water.

Watching the old man fuss with the water jars, I recalled stories of travellers in days past who relied on shelter and water such as this as they journeyed through the countryside. To provide assistance to travellers had been a longstanding way for a Buddhist to make merit. I wondered how many years would pass before these traditional stands offering cool water would all be replaced by commercial vendors selling colas?

Soon three of his grandchildren appeared with enamelled food containers. The old man joined the children in front of their humble shop to wait silently for a monk to collect their alms.

In a few minutes a monk came along the lane and stopped in front of them. All stepped out of their sandals, walked forward and put rice and some curries in the monk's bowl. Then, in unison, they all knelt and wai-ed to the monk. They remained kneeling until the monk turned away.

Another monk approached the gate, his alms collecting apparently completed for the day. A middle-aged Thai lady, neatly groomed in her ankle-length skirt so popular in the north, appeared from nowhere and called softly to him. He stopped at the call of her voice and turned around, keeping his eyes downcast. As he pulled back his robe to reveal his bowl, she hurried toward him carrying a reed tray filled with what appeared to be rice sweets packaged in green banana leaves and three white lotus buds. He took the lid from his bowl while she slipped out of her shoes before placing the food and flowers in his bowl. When she finished, she knelt on the ground and wai-ed.

He never looked at her, nor spoke to her. He slowly took the flowers from his bowl in order to put the lid back on and, with the flowers and bowl tucked beneath his robes, he, also, turned toward the gate.

The woman had made merit by giving food to the monk. The monk, in turn, was doing a good deed by being available so that the woman could make merit by giving him food. He was in no way begging.

And so it was – as it had been for centuries – the faithful providing food, medicine, clothing, and shelter for the monks, who, in turn, instruct others about the teachings of Buddha, teach the children, and provide counsel and wisdom to the lay people.

The man who gives alms today may be a monk himself tomorrow. It is expected that all young men will enter the monkhood for some period – a few weeks, a few months, years, or a lifetime – and most do enter, many for the three-month, Rains Retreat period.

As I watched other monks returning along the lane, I recalled the Thai Air Force pilot, an old acquaintance of mine, who felt that he could never marry until he had been a monk. He believed that he was unfit for marriage until he had learned an understanding of life that the discipline and study of a monk could provide.

As other monks returned from their morning alming rounds, I wondered how many would be leaving the wat to return to secular life. I certainly couldn't know by looking at their serene faces. It has always seemed much more difficult to be ordained into the monkhood than to leave it. In addition to elaborate ceremonies that often require days of preparation by the family, the individual must prove that he is not in debt, is not escaping family responsibilities, and is not a criminal.

To leave the monkhood, the monk has to do little more than announce his plans to disrobe to the Abbot and other monks. In some cases there are elaborate disrobing ceremonies. There is little pressure on monks to stay in the monkhood. One leaves at his own will, with no dishonour whatsoever. I was reminded again of the individualistic nature of these Theravada Buddhists.

I decided that I had better return to my quarters until I discovered the rules of Wat Muang Mang.

On my porch, I watched monks returning from alming walk to a water faucet to wash off their feet before returning to their guti to eat their morning food. At this same faucet young novices and temple boys were gathered to fill earthen waterjugs. To help keep insects out of the drinking water, there was an improvised system that filtered the water through three vats, each at a lower level. It seemed a slow process, but it was important for this water to be filtered since everyone in the wat, except perhaps the temple boys, had vowed to refrain from killing any living creature.

Soon activities ceased and the wat became quiet. Everyone was undoubtedly eating – except me. It didn't really matter; I was no longer hungry. But I wondered how I was going to get food. I had some bananas, but they would not last for long. Finally I decided it was useless to worry about these mundane problems too much. Somehow it would all work out.

With food off my mind for the moment, I looked at the physical lay-out of the compound for the first time.

The long porch of the women's quarters resembled quarters for Texas ranch hands – a long row of small adjoining rooms with an extended roof overhanging a walkway common to all rooms. I counted seven rooms and for a few moments I speculated on the female inhabitants cloistered within.

This small and compact compound was simple and clean. One large old building, where the novices seemed to be living, was made of teakwood and weathered chocolate brown by torrential monsoon rains, the sun, and the ages. It reminded me of the teaching hall at Wat Sraket in Bangkok, though not nearly so grand. This building leaned, twisted, and humped-up in odd places making it resemble a giant and aged beast. Large pieces of saffron cloth, the robes of novices, draped from the second storey windows gave a festive air to the rambling and crooked building.

Along the high white-washed brick wall surrounding the wat compound, were towering palm trees and lacy lumyai trees. Near the entrance was a fragile and spindly 'bodhi' tree – the kind of tree under which the Indian Prince Siddhartha

Gautama was sitting when he reached enlightenment. The bodhi tree was protected by a fence festooned with faded strips of saffron cloth.

Since all the monks seemed to be occupied with their morning meals, I decided that it was a good time to visit the 'viharn', a large temple hall where lay people worship before statues of Buddha.

This viharn seemed fairly new. A twinkling facade of blue and green glasswork was the background for a large three-headed elephant which was positioned majestically as the principal design on the facade. I kicked off my shoes before entering a cool darkness. Candles flickered on altars beneath a giant sitting Buddha casting light on its hands and face. I knelt on the straw mats. As my eyes became accustomed to the dimness, I noticed that the walls were painted in scenes from the Jataka Tales, stories of the many lives of the Buddha. I also noticed that behind the Buddha statue was a halo made of a metallic substance. I had never seen this effect before. Usually the statues are simple and serene without much artistic flourish.

When I stood up to leave, I heard a strange noise in the dark corner by the door. For a moment, I froze! What was over there? I peered into the darkness until I recognized the forms of two sleeping men. One was snoring slightly. With a sigh of relief, I quietly slipped past them. They were undoubtedly travellers who had sought shelter for the night. Usually travellers sleep in the 'sala', a pleasant open-air structure that generally has only a roof and floor. I wondered why they were asleep in the viharn?

Outside I sat on the viharn steps and was quickly surrounded by a dozen mangy temple dogs who proceeded to have a wonderful time sniffing the newcomer. I tried not to look at the poor beasts, most of whom were covered with sores oozing pus. Occasionally I caught momentary glimpses of saffron robes fluttering among the guti that semi-circled the viharn. This signalled that the monks were finished with their morning meal. I decided that I should return to my room to practise meditation.

Before I could begin, a temple boy tapped ever so lightly on my window calling, 'Khaow Tom', boiled rice soup. I went to the door to be presented with a two-pint capacity yellow enamelled bowl brimming with soup.

Boiled rice has a peculiarly pungent smell, sometimes quite overwhelming in the early morning hours, but this morning it smelled a bit better than usual. Listlessly, I stirred the heavy soup. One thing that I have never gotten accustomed to, even after so many years of living in Asia, is a breakfast of rice soup. Somehow eggs or fruit have much more appeal. I ate as much of the rice gruel as possible, about half of it. But what was I to do with the remaining half? I couldn't leave it in my room to attract a collection of many-legged scavengers. Then I noticed mae-chee walking by my room. They were going somewhere with their enamelled bowls – empty.

How silly I felt not knowing how to handle a most mundane aspect of wat life. So I tried eating more rice soup, but it was useless. Then I got the idea that I would dispose of the remaining porridge by washing it down the toilet. Just as I was cleaning out the last particles of rice, I suddenly remembered that this was probably an open sewer, as so many were in Thailand, and that someone would likely notice that the farang woman was throwing away good food – food that I later learned was given to the wat for female meditators and novices, by the faithful as a means of making merit. But the warning came too late.

Soon after morning rice, I heard a swishing, rustling sound which was dotted with light chatter. I looked outside to see the wat bustling with brooms made of gangly dried grasses. While some lively novices were gaily cleaning their sleeping quarters in the aged brown building, there was another detail sweeping the sandy courtyard. I walked outside to find that each mae-chee was silently sweeping her room and the spot of veranda in front of her cell. Looking around, I observed that there were five white-clad mae-chee, the old humped-back lady, and me – the farang. Not only had I discovered the identity of the other females, but I had discovered another wat routine – after morning gruel comes cleaning. So I joined in with my broom. By the time that I had my room swept and was ready to work on my part of the veranda, the mae-chee were already finished and out of sight.

I stood on the porch with my broom looking around the compound for the Abbot, but I saw no heads with a slight Friar Tuck fringe. I was hoping that someone might see me loitering about the porch with nothing to do and report it to the Abbot. What was I supposed to be doing? Here I was in a meditating wat standing rather stupidly with a broom in my hands, not having the slightest idea how to practise this new kind of meditation.

I kept a watch for the Abbot until most of the monks and novices had retired to their quarters for study and meditation. Then I decided to do the same.

As I prepared to begin my meditation, I felt uncomfortable practising samadhi meditation in a vipassana centre. I didn't know if there were a way that an observer could ascertain what method of meditation I was using. Finally, I convinced myself that this kind of thinking was ridiculous and I began concentrating on breathing-in and breathing-out. As my medi-tation was ending, I heard a woman's voice in Thai asking 'What's she doing?'

A hushed answer followed, 'She's practising vipassana.'

I turned toward the window to see one of the mae-chee, with her hands cupped around her eyes, peeping in at me to report to the others on the activities of the farang woman.

I was amused by their 'peeping Tom' behaviour, yet I knew it wasn't fair to label it as that. They were curious, but also concerned about this newcomer in their midst. I was also relieved that they thought I was practising vipassana!

It wasn't until after the last food of the day, which was delivered about 11:00 am, that I met the other female medi-tators face-to-face.

This time I ate all my food, which consisted of a large mound of rice topped with a bit of beef curry and boiled green vegetables. When the white-clad women paraded before my room, I joined the tail-end of the procession with an empty plate. The slow procession stopped at the end of the veranda where a giant vat of water stood.

Six Thai women, including the hunch-backed lady, gathered to wash their dishes. Three had shaved heads; two did not, but they all wore white. The old lady, whom I later learned was homeless, wore a faded blue blouse and a worn blue print sarong.

I was glad that I was wearing a white blouse and my light yellow sarong, which seemed appropriate enough.

Over the washing and rinsing of our tin plates, they asked my name and where I came from. They spoke slowly and smiled often. One young mae-chee, whose delicate features were attenuated by her shaved head, asked me if I was going to shave my head.

All eyes rested on me, waiting for my answer. Hesitantly I explained that I had just had it cut short, about one inch all over my head. That didn't seem to be enough of an explanation. So I told them that my sister had asked me *not* to shave it off because she was to be married soon and didn't want her sister bald at the wedding. They giggled and for the moment the question died.

I had cut my hair as short as possible hoping that it would not be outrageously against the rules, but I was also prepared to have it shaved if necessary. I had been told before coming to the wat that female meditators were not allowed to wear nail polish, perfume, lipstick, or jewelry.

My hair seemed to be a point of teasing. Later on several mae-chee, in jest, would occasionally suggest that I shave my head.

For the moment, I was determined to be the last to finish the simple dish-washing task which I thought took far too much time for such an easy chore. I loitered at the water vat so I could see what they did with their dishes. As they walked away to place them in a drying rack on the veranda, I observed how strange their movements were. It took one woman minutes to walk the short distance from the dish-washing apparatus to her room. She walked as if she might be ill or crippled. Later I would learn from personal experience that this slowness of all physical actions was a natural attitude that one assumed when in intensive meditation.

The pre-monsoon sun raged overhead making life on earth miserable. There was little breeze and the hot air clung to my body. I sat on the floor trying to meditate. I had reasoned that meditating might be the only release from the oppressive heat and from my mounting anxieties. I felt as if I had been abandoned, left to melt in cell number four.

Soon after the 5:00 pm gong calling the monks to chant, a voice near my window called my name. It was the novice who spoke English. He, of course, couldn't enter my room, so I went outside to him. He told me that the Abbot was ready to see me for my first lesson. At last, I was to learn something of vipassana meditation!

We went together to the steps of the viharn to join other people who were also waiting to talk with the Abbot. With scrubbed faces and clean clothes, some of the faithful of this wat sat on the steps before the viharn whose glasswork motif was glittering with the radiant art of the setting sun as it touched the wat for the last time this day.

Soon the Abbot appeared and all those on the steps wai-ed low to him. He motioned the novice and me to follow him into a wooden building near the viharn. It was an old building in similar condition to the 'aged-beast' building. This one appeared to be used as a classroom. There were small tables, undersized wood chairs, one portable blackboard, several bare light bulbs hanging from the ceiling, and numerous pictures of monks, the wat, government officials, and the Thai King and Queen on the walls.

I sat down at one of the tables and the Abbot sat at another one in front of me. The novice went to the blackboard. The first lesson began.

Upon the Abbot's instructions, the novice wrote on the blackboard and then interpreted for me a brief description of each of the four basic foundations.

## VIPASSANA (Insight Meditation)

Four Foundations of Mindfulness
   I. Body (Kaya)
      Rightness (right step, left step, rising, falling)
   II. Feeling (Vedana)
      Pain, sickness, happiness, unhappiness, suffering
   III. Mind (Citta)
      Thinking, restless mind
   IV. Teachings (Dhamma)
      Likes, dislikes, sleepiness, restfulness, doubts, phenomena, awareness of movements, fleeting mind.

After the theoretical part of the lesson was completed which I had not understood at all, the Abbot asked the novice to stand up on one of the larger tables. With the novice as a demonstration model, the Abbot explained the first steps involved in practising vipassana meditation.

First he asked the novice to squat down in the position assumed by one getting ready to wai. The novice stooped down slowly and deliberately like one doing calisthenics in slow motion.

Then he asked the novice to demonstrate with his hands. Very slowly, the young boy wrapped in saffron moved first his right hand and then his left from his chest to his forehead, then back to his chest, and finally he lowered each hand, the right first, to the floor with the little finger side of the hand touching first and then the palm rolling to touch the floor.

After the novice had slowly demonstrated this with both hands, he put his forehead to the floor in such a manner that his thumbs seemed to be touching between his eyebrows. The novice said little, he seemed to be concentrating. And I could only barely understand the Abbot's instructions.

When this demonstration was completed, the Abbot turned to me and asked me if I understood. I respectfully placed my hands to my face in a position of respect and simply answered 'Yes'. But, in truth, I didn't really understand.

As we talked, the novice repeated this hand action very slowly and deliberately. Sometime during the third repetition of this slow manoeuvre, I realized what he was doing. The young man was demonstrating the wai that the faithful give to show respect to monks and to Buddha images, but he was doing it in a form broken apart and separated so that each movement became an individual act.

I learned, at last, that the three wai which had troubled me so in the past were not only designed to show respect to the Buddha, his teachings, and the brotherhood of monks, but in this meditation wat, this exercise was implemented to teach the meditator to concentrate on his bodily movements. For the Buddhist, it was a natural exercise, but to me without such knowledge it had seemed a bit bizarre.

Distracted by my sudden understanding of the wai, I didn't have time to memorize the exact movements involved in this meditational wai.

Next, the Abbot requested the novice to stand, reminding him to be aware. After standing erect with his eyes looking straight ahead, the novice put his hands behind his back with his right over his left. Then he lifted his right foot slowly and placed it down slowly just inches ahead of his left foot. The Abbot leaned over to measure with his fingers the distance between the novice's two feet. The novice had taken too big a step, so he scooted his foot back a bit, while explaining that the proper distance between the feet was the space equal to four fingers.

With his stance corrected, the novice began walking again, ever so slowly. As he neared the end of the table, he teetered a bit as the table, wrongly weighted, almost sent him sprawling. But he recovered to initiate a turn which was always to the right, performed in a small square with heels touching throughout the turn. With the turn completed, he began with the right foot, lifting and putting down each foot in slow, snail-like movements.

The Abbot next instructed his model to sit, reminding him to be mindful of sitting. After the novice had straightened his robes and moved his body about to a comfortable position, he

placed his hands, the right over the left, in the open space between his crossed legs. The Abbot then picked up the boy's
robes to show me the proper position of the legs. The right
heel should be touching the long, frontal leg bone of the
left leg, thus putting the left leg on the inside.

The novice sat immobile, his eyes closed, and his body
relaxed. He was beautiful as he sat there on a wobbly table
amidst a room of empty tables and chairs.

The Abbot watched him closely and then explained that in
vipassana the meditator must be aware of his stomach's rising
and falling as he breathes. All concentration should be on
the stomach.

After a few minutes, the young novice opened his eyes and
climbed down from the table to interpret what the Abbot
was saying.

'If you practise all these forms, then you will have concentration. When you see things think – seeing, seeing, seeing.
Your assignment for tonight and tomorrow is to practise these
techniques. Practise sitting and walking meditation for five or
ten minutes or whatever time you can. Make a conscious
effort to lift the foot and bring it down again and bring the
mind to the stomach. Be aware of every movement, every
muscle, every touch – all the time. Even when you are eating,
be aware of tasting. If you want to leave your room, you
may walk inside the compound, but you must always be
mindful. Be aware constantly – be mindful.'

The Abbot watched me as I scanned my notes, and then
announced, 'You will report to either me or the chief meditating monk each evening between five and six o'clock.'

With that pronouncement, I realized that my first lesson
was finished. I stood, wai-ed low once, muttered a thank-you,
and left to return to my cell. As I crossed the compound, the
novice hurried after me. 'Be mindful of your steps. You're
walking too fast to be mindful of what you are doing. In
vipassana you must be mindful all the time.'

I sat on my bed allowing the gathering shadows to enclose
me in my cell so I could think. Not only was I a bit put-down
by the novice's criticism and annoyed by hunger, but I was

confused about the meaning of the four foundations of vipassana. The Abbot had gone over these foundations so quickly
that I wondered if they were unimportant. This seemed un-
likely, but he had seemed to concentrate more on the physical
techniques involved.

Still feeling sorry for myself, I wondered why I was having
such difficulties comprehending philosophical instruction from
Buddhist teachers. As I reflected on the lesson, I thought of
the Abbot who with concern and patience had instructed me
while a growing group of people had gathered outside to see
him. I decided that he possessed 'chai yen', a cool heart, or a
heart detached, a trait much admired among Thais. Yet, at
the same time, he exhibited compassion.

I was back again to the same puzzle – how can there be
detached compassion? I could see it in others, but I could not
yet know it within myself.

In addition to the mystery of detachment, I still had to
come to grips with constant mindfulness. How many times
did he say – 'Be mindful!' What was this mindfulness? Was
it to observe people and things more carefully? This I always
had thought was something that I did fairly well, being a
writer. Buddhist mindfulness seemed to be something more.
Was it to be more conscious of one's self? I decided that it
could not be that since one of the goals of meditation was
to eliminate the importance of 'I'. What, then, was this
mindfulness?

As I troubled over a possible meaning, a ponderous thought
invaded my thinking. Maybe mindfulness demanded 'chai
yen' – detachment? If that were true, then I would never
know mindfulness.

A splattering of moonlight penetrating through the trees
littered the floor with leafy footprints that moved just ahead
of mine as I practised walking meditation. Then I settled
down into the exotic patterns to try sitting meditation. Try
as I did, though, it seemed impossible to divert my attention
from breathing-in and breathing-out of samadhi to the rising
and falling of my stomach practised in vipassana.

After a protracted effort, I concluded that I was neither able to be mindful nor to practise vipassana. I remained hunched on the floor a heap of despondence, until I remembered the old Abbot at Wat Bovornives' sage advice – be patient, be gentle with your mind. So I began again. I walked, wai-ed in slow motion and sat until the entire universe seemed asleep. Even the moon patterns on the floor had gone.

At last, I lay on the bed, tired but no longer hungry. I had learned that water consumed slowly subdues hunger. I was no longer apprehensive about my dismal failures. I was learning that patience could subdue anxiety.

I fell asleep to be awakened by the 4:00 gong and the accompanying chorus of wailing dogs. The chanting, ancient and profound, seemed to be echoing from centuries past, to inspire me to try again to meditate in the way of vipassana.

After a relatively more successful attempt to meditate, I sat on the veranda to watch the monks give shape and form to a dusky dawn as they flowed through the gates to collect alms. Then came the rice soup, followed by the tasks of washing my bowl and myself, and cleaning my cell. Then more attempts at meditation, noon rice, more meditation, insufferable heat, the 5:00 gong, reporting to the meditation monk, and more meditation.


The nagging questions concerning wat routines and women's restrictions were soon resolved. I discovered that I could go anywhere in the compound except the 'bot', a small building adjacent to the viharn in which the vows of monkhood were given. Of course, I never entered a monk's guti, except the guti of the Abbot. I did walk among the guti, but it wasn't a wise venture for a woman. Often the monks would be bathing or relaxing in the privacy of their guti with their robes loosened to a degree that they thought was not proper for a woman's eyes. Perhaps their legs or their chests would be revealed and they would be embarrassed.

As I became more at home in Wat Muang Mang, I began to retreat from the heat of my room to sit on the veranda or the viharn steps and try to be mindful.

Throughout the day, men and women, young and old, came to the viharn to offer flowers, incense, and prayers before the Buddha. They came in silence, knelt in silence, and left without utterance.

I also became aware not only of an increasing number of lay people coming and going as they planned ordination ceremonies for their sons, brothers, or grandsons, but of neighbourhood children, not always silent, who used the sandy courtyard as a playground.

This considerable activity in the wat, a meditating wat, seemed unnatural and for me was most distracting. Yet as I watched the mae-chee, as they cared for the flowers and prepared food for the temple boys and other mae-chee, or as I watched the monks moving about doing their chores, counselling lay people, or teaching scriptures to the novices, I became aware that all these activities were done in un-hurried, graceful movements which were accompanied by a sense of serenity – of a lack of burden.

As I watched them I wondered if I would ever come to know 'chai yen', cool heart, or mindfulness?

It didn't seem possible that I ever would.

## Chapter Eight

Westerners are born with books:
Thais are born with experience.
Interpreter at Wat Muang Mang

AND the world fell away. I don't know when it happened, or just how. There was no 'satori', sudden enlightenment; no particular wisdom whispered to me by meditation teachers; no mystical rites nor esoteric readings. But my world changed.

I don't know where it all began. Maybe it did not begin; maybe it was always there beyond my awareness.

When I encountered decaying, decomposing human bodies in my meditation, did I begin to have some understanding that impermanence is omnipotent and irrevocable? When various parts of my body, hurting and appearing grotesquely disproportioned, seemed to possess the total energy of my existence, did I experientially understand that pain and suffering dominate human life? When I walked with no legs or drifted beyond space, time, and knowledge of 'me', was this an insight into 'anatta' – the concept that there is no constant 'I' or 'me'.

I can draw no conclusions. For, as I was constantly reminded, one must be wary of delusion and ignorance which constantly confuse one's ability to see the truth.

With a typical Western attitude, I constantly wanted to know, ahead of time, what might happen to me, if anything, in intensive meditation.

I worried about my inability to understand the concept of vipassana. What was it? Insight, I was told. Insight into what? In a vague answer, I was told that it was only through vipassana that I could gain an understanding of dhamma, Buddha's teachings; that through developing an awareness of the physical body, an awareness of feeling, an awareness of consciousness or the mind, I could know something of the nature of mental states and matter and how they are constantly and rapidly arising and falling away – so fast, in fact, that they seem to be permanent entities. Thinking that mental states and matter are permanent is delusion. I was told that through vipassana I would come to know all of this. This understanding of the nature of reality could not be known from books nor lectures; it could only be known through one's self, one's own experiences and insights. It was only through the practice of vipassana, I was reminded, that one could eventually obtain nibbana, a release from the wheel of life and rebirth and thus from suffering.

To my troubled questions a Thai nurse who became my regular interpreter would often reply : 'You must learn from experience. You Westerners are handicapped in your pursuit of truth. Westerners are born with books; Thais are born with experience.'

Finally I began to see that I was not being patient enough and that I was *wanting* to know and wanting excessively,

which is undesirable. It was hard to remember that the present was more important than either the future or the past. It seemed that I would never find any of the answers if I persisted in my querulous questionings. I knew that I must follow the advice of those who had spent lifetimes in saffron learning the secrets of this discipline. If I could follow their instructions perhaps, I, too, would come to know the truths of which they spoke.

So I stopped struggling with intellectual problems and settled down somewhat patiently in my austere cell in a simple, small wat which provided two simple rice meals, one taken early in the morning and another about 11:00, the last food of the day. This routine of meditation and awareness-practice appeared on the surface so simple, and in no way suggested the dramatic experiences that were to come about in these limited physical facilities and through an unencumbered, simple routine of life.

While the intellectual quandaries were shelved, there were other strains and troubles. In addition to the struggle of keeping all eight precepts, which included learning enough restraint to brush away mosquitoes sucking my blood, there were the problems of insufferable heat, the overwhelming toilet odours, and the horrendous noises of motorcycles and the quarrelsome dogs. But troublesome as these petty nuisances were, they were ultimately inconsequential compared to the awesomeness of meditation.

Meditation exercises were relatively simple at first. Initially, the walking meditation stressed awareness of lifting the right foot and then the left one. Later on, awareness was directed to the lifting, holding, pressing of the legs and feet – to become aware of all muscles and nerves involved in conducting the manoeuvres of taking a step. This was often accompanied by unusual pain or discomfort, often in areas not usually associated with walking.

Initially, the focus of sitting meditation involved centering concentration on the stomach's rising and falling. This created a conflict for me. My concentration seemed bound to a mindfulness of the air coming and going through my nose, following the technique I had been taught at Wat Bovornives. Then one morning in my walking meditation my consciousness shifted to my stomach's rising and falling.

As I was walking, I became aware that my legs were missing. The process of walking was not obvious. I was also very aware of my eyes, back, neck, and heart; they ached. My whole being was composed of two organs, the eyes and the heart, and a backbone that extended into a neck.

With the walking meditation completed, I began concentrating on the slow-motion wai which I did three times before each sitting meditation. Then I found a comfortable sitting position and began to try to focus on my stomach's rising and falling.

That day, the struggle to bring my awareness away from my nose to my stomach seemed less difficult, particularly when the blue hues emerged. These familiar tones remained only briefly. This blueness quickly converted into a floating luminescence touched with light yellow. This fluff of frosted gossamer gently swirled about in such a way that an aura of light, so delicate, so fragile, conveyed happiness. It was an ethereal effervescence of joy that shimmered and beckoned. Then these clouds of white plunged into a darkish rusty red, only to soar once again into white mountains and valleys of serenity.

At some point I became aware that there was a tremendous force encircling my navel. There was a ring around my navel to which were attached the muscles of the rest of my body. With the rising and falling, the muscles attached to this ring touched and tugged on other muscles throughout my body as if this ring were the master control – like a puppeteer's rig from which a puppet is manipulated.

As the rising and falling continued, my white undulating world collected together into a more solid form and plummeted into blood-red pools. Plumes of heroic blue waved from the edges of the shimmering red lava pools. Eventually the blue plumage conquered the crater. In the calmness of blue, meditation ended.

I was aware that a critical struggle had ceased. From then on, it would be easier to be aware of the stomach's rising and falling.

It was not long before I became aware that my movements were almost unconsciously deliberate and slow, that I was spending up to eighteen hours a day either meditating or trying to be mindful, that I spent less than one hour a day talking and that my books held no interest for me. Time, in the traditional sense, no longer existed for me. A day could pass in minutes or was it an eternity?

The nimitta (acquired sign) appeared occasionally, but only briefly. It did not seem important any more whether it appeared or not. The blueness, soothing and tranquil, was there, but always in the background and I tried not to be interested in it.

I did not know why I practised meditation so much. Was it because the Abbot expected it of me? Or was it because there was so little else to do? Or was it because I was curious – or what? I lacked an explanation other than that I longed to meditate. Exceptional experiences and new dimensions awaited

me in meditation, or perhaps as a result of it. But there was more to this longing. Once the initial struggle of fixing concentration and stilling the mind was completed, there often followed a feeling of detachment that carried with it a calmness and tranquillity that I had never known.

Yet, seemingly incongruously, what happened during meditation was often neither calm nor tranquil.

An eye, one eye, was watching me. A glittering eye which had emerged from fields of azure moved quickly through the vast space toward me. As the eye came nearer, the blues, as if aware of their creation, kaleidoscoped about the eye. But then the eye, becoming dominant, pressed the blues into darker and darker shades until all was a blackness that decreased considerably the vastness of my world.

At first it seemed to be a cat's eye, but as it came nearer, I recognized it as a human eye, an oriental one, slanted, observing, omniscient, and benign. Singularly, it rested before me in hushed aquamarine, a startling contrast against the black and restricting purdah veil that curtained my world from view.

The eye was never stationary. I could never look at it directly to the exclusion of all else. If I should I knew that it would disappear. Without warning, the shivering eye receded into the purdah darkly, diminishing in size as it retreated. The ebony coloured half-sphere became even deeper in colour and the blackness of its strength pushed against the dome-like limits of my horizon, expanding my world once again. The purdah had been lifted.

Again, without warning, I observed someone sitting before me in this immense universe of darkness. The figure, shadowy and almost unrecognizable, was male, old, frail, and oriental.

While being aware, at least partially, of the old man, I was suddenly overwhelmed with an exuberant gush of freedom, lightness, and happiness. Then, just as unexpectedly, there was nothing. Then there appeared the face of another, or the same, old oriental man. A smile revealed one snaggled tooth. As I watched, the face began to change, to become even older; only the single snaggle tooth remained static. Then the face froze, as if in death; the skull began to decay, to wither away. The eyes disappeared; the skin tightened. Only the tooth remained unaltered.

My body was flushed, tingling with a heat that was fearful. I was under-going shock of some kind. The prickling heat burned me so fiercely that the mass of my body became an odd-shaped ball of smouldering fire without flames. It was painful and exhausting, or so it seemed, yet there was also the calm awareness of the stomach's rising and falling.

The prickling heat eventually became less poignant and in the ensuing warmness, meditation ended.

After recording this experience in my notebook, and not yet feeling the need for sleep, I went outside to the veranda to watch and listen to the monks and mae-chee settle in for the night. Soon everything was quiet; the birds were silent and even the dogs were hushed.

As I sat there looking at the stars and the sliver of moon, I knew for a fleeting moment that the quiet that existed inside me was greater than the quiet of the surroundings. It was a bittersweet moment; a precious and tender moment that could never be caressed nor repeated. Never!

I reflected that life was full of the bittersweet. So many feeling moments in life appear spontaneously, but before they can be consummated, they disappear. Some reappear in altered forms as floating dots in time only to dissolve again. It is truly bittersweet, this lifetime of pursuing bubbles of joy that only burst when neared.

I thought of my bittersweet puzzle of Christmas Days. For weeks, with tremendous eagerness, exuberance, and prep-aratory activities, I anticipate, not necessarily the day, but the joy the day is to bring. Without fail, the glittering anticipation fades and is in shreds before the occasion matures. Why, I've asked myself so many times, is this so?

It all seemed so clear to me as I sat alone beneath an ebony sky laden with crystalline reminders of unlimited universes. Thinking seemed so easy this night. My mind seemed able to examine thoughts within a long, narrow tunnel in which only one idea at a time existed.

I understood that I was unprepared culturally to live in the present. When the future, the anticipation, was no longer lingering on, there was only the present. But my world had never been oriented to the present, only in this wat had I learned of existing in the present which was an entirely new experience.

In time I returned to my room to lie down on my rigid bed, whereupon an unparalleled seven hours followed.

During sleep it seemed as if I were in meditation, or was it the other way around? My body did not touch the bed; it floated just centimetres above it. When I turned over, I knew the precise movements that my body would make, particularly my hands and arms. The usual discomforts that usually occurred when I put weight on previously bruised and now sensitive bones were absent. Since my body was tranquilly suspended, there was no pain. I was aware that I was sleeping, yet it wasn't normal sleeping. It was much more than that; it was extreme relaxation and serenity created by a knowledge that my mind and body were in harmony. This feeling continued until the four o'clock morning gong.

The next day in meditation, the slanted eye returned. It was born from a melange of luminous colours and dull, muted greys. It was a knowing eye, similar to the first eye. It observed me, calmly and carefully. Then it became part of the misty greys. Suddenly there was someone looking directly into my eyes at very close range, seemingly only inches away. The brilliant eyes observed, dulled, and then were no longer eyes, just eye sockets. A blackness rushed from the depths of the skeletal sockets smothering all else. From the ebony pits came another single slanted eye which looked, saw, and then disintegrated into the sterile grey.

After meditation, I wondered again how many minds I had. It seemed that I was not only aware of the eye, albeit in another distinct but distant level, but that I also acknowledged the ticking of my wrist-watch (about seven feet away on the small table). And, it seemed that I had been aware of the rising and falling of my diaphragm.

Did I have several minds? Or, if I didn't, then was it possible that I had unknown senses that remained dormant under 'normal circumstances'? Or was my mind, in some way, able to separate things, feelings, or whatever, to acknowledge each in isolation? I did not know, but I was distinctly aware that my mind had many more dimensions than I had known of four months ago.

At the reporting session that night, the chief meditating monk explained that the previous night's all-night meditation was due to the lasting powers of concentration. He explained that this strong power of concentration was good, desirable, maybe even progress.

Again I commented on the incomprehensible passage of time. From his regally carved chair, he looked down at me with a smile and glance that told me that he also knew such feelings. His warm response was simply, 'Excellent'.

Intently he looked down upon me as I told him of last evenings deteriorating skull which had startled and maybe even threatened me. After reflecting for some time on my descriptions of the disintegrating slanted eyes into decayed skulls, he sagely responded. 'Only those who practise vipassana can know the impermanence of all things. All things arise and fall – arise and fall. All things. Man, too.'

Another day passed outside of time, yet I was acutely aware of my environment, myself, and the changes occurring within myself. I was particularly aware of physical changes and wrote of them in my notebook.

Hunger, as I once understood it, no longer exists. Eating is a mindful task and not an attempt to subdue the hunger need as quickly as possible.

I eat no food from approximately 11:00 am until 6:00 am the next day – 19 hours without food, yet there is no great hunger. Water sipped slowly is just as satisfying as food.

While hunger seems to be absent, I'm plagued by extraordinary feelings of physical exhaustion. This fatigue seems purely physical. My mind is not only constantly alert, but seemingly more incisive. Although I sleep only a few hours a night, both my mind and body seem to enter deep stages of restfulness. It's interesting that I have no dreams during intensive meditation.

While the chief meditating monk responds to my complaints of tiredness with 'excellent', the Abbot tells me that a meditator feels physical tiredness because the act of meditation can consume vast energies. Upon first thoughts, this seems a paradox. In intensive meditation, physical activities and motions are drastically curtailed and slowed-down, or so it seems. Is it possible that it requires more energy in learning to still the mind than in allowing it to flit about unknowingly?

I am now aware that I, too, walk and move in what I once considered to be a ridiculous manner. I'm wondering if I resemble the white-clad mae-chee who, to me, seemed to move like wind-up bride dolls?

Obvious changes are occurring within me. Are they the result of altered dimensions of perception? Recently, these changes have seemed voluntary and natural, yet mystifying. I am not afraid.

Has my physical appearance also changed during this time of intensive meditation? It seems possible, but there are no mirrors, so I can't see. Is this absence of mirrors deliberate? Probably not, just not considered essential.


Concentration during meditation on the rising and falling of my stomach was easier. Soothing blues often filled my universe with shapes of such intricate designs and hues of such radiance and sublimity that they remain unnamed in our world.

One afternoon the blues created and vibrated until they coagulated into minute circular forms that began to breathe. As they breathed, they became larger and more distinct. In time I recognized that they were human body cells. They continued breathing and expanding for some time, then they gradually disintegrated, stopped breathing, and turned brown.

After the death of the cells, a heavy monsoon rain moved swiftly across my universe. The dead cells, now miniscule and grey, were lost in the soft, soothing, and mute rains. The rains ceased and more blue cells were born, only to grow, to die, and to be consumed by the calming rains. This life cycling seemed to be repeating itself throughout centuries of time. I was aware that the process was natural and flowing. There was an absence of any violent thrashing about to alter the flow; there was only acceptance.

As meditation softly ended, a buzzer-type bell which called each meditator to a reporting session was ringing eight times, calling the mae-chee from cell eight. In the coolness of evening each mae-chee and myself, one by one, upon being called, would walk thoughtfully and slowly to a small cement and stone building constructed somewhat like a cave which nestled among the lacy lumyai trees and the wooden guti. Here, in incense-laden coolness, meditators came to report troubles, pains, and progress to the chief meditating monk, who was referred to as the 'second Abbot'.

My turn to report either to the chief meditating monk or to the Abbot, who was reverently called 'Acharn', or teacher, usually came just before dark. Tonight darkness was imminent and still I hadn't been called. As I sat alone on the veranda, I thought that the farang might have been forgotten. I decided to walk to the viharn steps hoping that my interpreter might be there to explain why I hadn't been called.

I saw her sitting on the viharn steps, her white nurse's uniform stark against the gathering dusk. This diminutive Thai woman was a former mae-chee and a long-standing student of the Abbot. In time I learned that after a short tenure as a foreign scholarship student studying advanced nursing in a New York City hospital, she had returned to Thailand and married a Thai man who, shortly after their marriage, was tragically killed. Then some time after his death, she became a mae-chee. In time her mother and friends convinced her that she should share with others the knowledge gained through her Buddhist study and meditation. Now she was back to nursing in the Chiang Mai Hospital and in her spare time acted as the official interpreter for Wat Muang Mang.

I loved this woman, whose wonderfully glowing smile and hushed voice met me each evening. She was gentle and compassionate in her understanding of my trials, troubles, questionings and joys in meditation; yet, she was so strong in her urgings to be aware, to be mindful, and to practise meditation with wisdom.

Eventually, we sat together on the cool floor before the meditation master who wore dark robes of burnt saffron. As usual, he sat cross-legged on a wooden chair resembling a howdah. Candles and incense smouldering on a small altar in one corner provided the only light. I, indeed, had not been forgotten. It was only that other meditators had taken longer than usual to discuss their progress.

As was customary, the reporting session was prefaced with me, the meditator, wai-ing three times very slowly, after which I told the monk of a cave of bones which I had repeatedly seen in my morning meditation and of the unending regeneration of body cells which I was aware of in the afternoon meditation.

He carefully explained that the bones and cells were an indication that body and mind, each separately, are all that exist. This monk, who had a distracted, far-away look in his eyes, a look much like that of the Abbot at Wat Bovornives, cautioned me not to concentrate on what I was seeing, but on the seeing itself; thus avoiding the defilements of wanting, liking, disliking, or clinging which hinder meditation progress.

As he contemplated my assignment for the next twenty-four hours, I wondered if meditators over the past twenty-five centuries had also seen body cells? The scientific discovery of a human cell with its components was knowledge of recent times. If ancient man did not know of human cells, then did he have visions of them or if he did, how did he understand them? Maybe he only saw blue circles that contracted, breathed, and disappeared. But if he saw cells, then was it not possible that some of the visions that I was having had more meaning than my small, undeveloped mind could comprehend?

Realizing that I was not supposed to be doing this kind of fanciful wondering into the past and future, I began to concentrate on 'thinking, thinking, thinking' to stay in the present until the monk announced my new lesson.

'Your next assignment is to think of rising, falling, sitting. Try to see the body, then try to see some parts of the body. Concentrate on hearing, seeing, smelling, touching, tasting. Remember,' he cautioned, 'do not look for sweet or sour when you taste, just be aware of tasting.'

As I wrote the assignment in my notebook, he watched. Then I wai-ed in the style expected of all meditators in this wat and backed into the darkness to return to my little cell to practise the new assignment as far into the night as possible.

Each day ended this way. The meditation monk or the Acharn seemed to have all the time and patience in the world to listen to me and to discuss my problems and questions. Any fear of either these two monks had disappeared as I became aware of their concern and compassion toward me.


As meditation practices became more complicated, my experiences became even more dramatic. At the same time, I felt an ever-increasing awareness of peace, calm and tranquillity. I was detached from space and time; this transcending of previously conceived boundaries was limitless, floating, ever-moving. It was similar to my feeling towards the nimitta: the nimitta was there and yet it wasn't. Was it because this awareness was so delicate . . . so ethereal that it couldn't be cradled? Was it my awareness of this tranquillity or was it as a result of it that bonds of insecurity broke, mundane troubles disappeared, the restrictions of self-centredness dissolved . . . leaving freedom.

One day I wrote in my notebook:

Time passes without knowledge. Strangest feeling – no interest in my old things. No interest in LAHU WILDFIRE (book I was writing at the time), nor my graduate work, nor can I feel the utter disgust and insanity that always arises when I think of the war and political intrigues over here. Nothing. Can't force myself to think about any of these. The only touch I seem to have with the outside, the world I once knew, is Buzz (my husband). I think of him only as a feeling; loving, happy, kind, but I don't think of him often.

Don't want to talk. Difficult to walk fast. Writing in my notebook is painful. Felt like crying in meditation this day. Mouth and eyes seemed to assume crying position, but there were no tears: at least I don't think so.

No desire to leave wat. Not hungry. Wonder why we are not allowed any stimulants like tea or coffee?

When there are no struggles, then there is a peace, a calmness unknown in any other kind of victory. It's freedom.

One afternoon after meditation I was sitting on my bed looking out the window at the young novices playfully washing their saffron robes and themselves at the large open well opposite the women's quarters. The first ripple of the wat gong, calling monks for chanting pierced my ears with a painful whining, high-pitched, unearthly sound. The temple dogs responded with their customary spine-tingling yelpings.

Waves from this shrieking gong sound reverberated in unbearable bursts against my ear drums, making me want to cry out, to howl like the temple dogs. At last, the monk stopped beating the gong, but the reverberating waves lingered on. Long thin slivers of sound continued to reach my ears for several more moments.

Once my hearing sense became more acute, I continued to hear sounds that were formerly denied me and probably are denied to most humans. In the stillness of the night, I could hear cockroaches moving about in my room. The first one I heard seemed to be in the far corner which was ten feet from me. With flashlight in hand, I investigated. There, in the circle of light was a cockroach clinging to a broom whisk. I heard them crawling in the toilet, along the floor, and in my belongings. Mindfully I would remember the precept not to kill, and manoeuvred them outside with my broom, but their replacements appeared almost immediately.

This increased ability to hear brought with it almost unbearable sensitivity to normally loud noises, such as the roar of motorcycles. I was told that by concentrating on 'hearing, hearing, hearing', the noise could be reduced to tolerable proportions. The advice was correct, but there was a great temptation to shut out the noise by ignoring it or by putting a protective covering over my ears, instead of concentrating on it.

Step by step it moved slowly up my arm. Whatever it was, it had numerous appendages which seemed to attach themselves to my skin with a prickly suction. It was large; its steps weighed heavily against my flesh.

I accepted the creature by concentrating on 'paining, paining, paining', as I continued breathing. At the conclusion of the meditation, I discovered that the mighty creature on my body was a tiny ant!

Often both my legs went to sleep during meditation. I do not know whether it was due to the longer sittings or caused by the more difficult positioning of my legs recommended by the Abbot. But I knew that after sitting meditation I would have to contend with numb legs. It became a habit to stretch them out in front of me after sitting meditation to allow the blood to flow properly again. One evening, after what had been a relaxed meditation, I straightened out my two numb appendages, but this time, although they were numb, the usual pain was absent. I became keenly aware of a gurgling noise in my right leg and a warmness. I could hear blood in my leg rushing into a multitude of veins and arteries, refilling them with warming blood. The sensation started just below my knee and worked its way downward in a criss-crossing that had no distinct pattern. Eventually, even the tiniest of blood vessels were lush once again with the warming blood – the numbness was gone. There was no pain during this time. In this state of heightened awareness it seemed possible to eliminate pain by becoming one with it and recognizing its nature.

All this and more had happened in a small pea-green room. There were no altars aglow with candles, no incense exotically perfuming the air, no monks sitting before me to encourage meditation. I sat alone, alone with myself exploring worlds and sensations previously unknown to me. There was no fear now; it all seemed natural.

Another memorable occasion occurred a few days before the Rains Retreat, known as 'Khaow Pansa'. I was sitting on the steps of the viharn when three old Thai women approached.

Their greying hair was cropped short like a man's, their colourful sarongs were brought up between their legs from behind so that it appeared they were wearing pantaloons. Their wrinkled and waxy skin shone from what appeared to be recent scrubbing. Their lips were reddened and their teeth blackened from years of chewing betel-nut.

They chattered away until they neared me, then their talk subsided while they observed me. Soon they decided to come over to talk. They wanted to know what I was doing in the wat. I explained that I was studying vipassana to which they responded 'riap rooy' – 'excellent'. Becoming more friendly, they sat down on the steps with me and we talked – we discussed the material of my blouse, my room number, the weather.

Then they told me that they were from a village miles away. They had come to Chiang Mai to 'tamboon' – to make merit – at this wat.

There followed a series of questions about vipassana and they concluded that it was a good thing to do, but none of them had done it yet. Now they thought they were too old. They pressed me to tell them what had happened in my meditation, but in my limited Thai I was unable to explain the extent of my experiences.

Finally, one old lady, looking me straight in the eyes, asked, 'Have you seen the phii?' (the spirits).

I should have guessed that the question would come, since most Thais are very interested in the phii. In the habit that I was now accustomed to, I hesitated a long time before forming an answer. They waited patiently.

I do not believe in ghosts, spirits, or phii, yet I could understand how they conceived that the images or visions of people in various forms of decomposition that one could see in a meditation experience, were phii. I knew that they believed in the phii, and had spirit houses near their homes to which they offered food, incense, and flowers to placate them.

Finally I had an answer. 'Farang can't see the phii, only Thais can see phii.'

And they laughed.

That seemed to satisfy them and soon they told me they must go inside the viharn to pay their respects. To my astonishment, all three of them got up, went back down the steps, knelt in front of me and wai-ed very low – to me – turned and climbed the steps to the viharn.

I watched the three old ladies whose dress, hair cuts, and probably their betel-nut chewing, the customs of ancient Siam, would die with them.

I thought about their belief in the phii. This belief in spirits and ghosts is an animistic carry-over from days prior to Buddhism and this, in turn, is influenced by the rites of ancestor worship. How easily these beliefs in spirits seem to merge with the belief in thirty-one worlds, only a few of whose beings humans can see. If the people believed this, then it seems natural to believe also that the phii not only exist, but are consistent with Buddhist thoughts, at least as understood by many lay people.

I began to wonder about the faces I had seen during meditation. I had seen faces not only during sitting meditation, but during walking meditation. Occasionally as I walked unfamiliar faces appeared as though they came from the walls of my room or rested among the leaves on the trees outside my cell. It would be easy to believe that those faces were phii.

The Thai also believe in the 'preta', the hungry ghosts, who exist in a lesser world than humans. These hungry ghosts are reborn as such because of their excessive greed in previous lives as humans. As a result, they are tormented in an existence plagued by unsatisfied cravings. Unable to communicate with people, the hungry ghosts cannot ask for food or possessions which they desire. They live long existences as preta, waiting until their bad kamma is exhausted, hoping that they will be reborn in human form. These hungry ghosts don't seem to harm people, only frighten them.

As I watched the old ladies sitting silently on straw mats before the viharn's giant Buddha, I wondered why these women had wai-ed to me in such a respectful way.

The next morning, I found at my door a small tray of homemade rice pastries artistically wrapped in green banana leaves. At first I ignored them, then the hunched-back lady came along. 'Take them. They're for you.'

'I don't understand,' I answered, knowing that there was no one to bring me extra food.

'They're for you,' she insisted waving her arm. 'Three old ladies brought them early this morning – for the farang woman in room number four who is studying vipassana.'

I picked up the tray and went inside. Were the old ladies being nice to me, the stranger? Or were they making merit by giving food to one who was studying vipassana? Or what? What a beautiful thing to do.

I reflected on the Buddhists' reverent respect for those among them who became monks, and the respect of a different kind that they showed to others who devote themselves to the learning of the dhamma and the practice of meditation. It was, after all, a goal of most Buddhists one day to join the monkhood, if a man, or practise meditation, if a woman.

Mindfully I ate a rice sweet and thought of the three old ladies whose gift had appeared so mysteriously at my door.

The instructions for sitting meditation had become more complicated. After the first few days, I was instructed to be aware of a touching on two spots on my lower back near the top edge of the thigh bone. I was told to think of it as if a coin were touching first the right bone and then the left. This was in addition to the awareness of the rising and falling of my diaphragm.

Later, two more points were added, making a total of four, plus the rising and falling. The new points were the buttocks bones, the ones that we sit on. Again it was an awareness of touching first the right side, then the left. It seemed to be a full circle . . . the two sides on the back, the two buttocks bones and the rising and falling.

There were the usual struggles at the beginning of these exercises to calm the mind, to initiate awareness in new places. Ironically the additional awareness points did not seem to make concentration or meditation appreciably more diffi-cult, once the pattern was established. But something else was happening. As awareness of these new concentration points sharpened, there was a lessening of knowledge of the existence of 'me'.

Parts of my body ceased to exist or to function. Sometimes various parts of my body became so pronounced that by their sheer magnitude obliterated all else. At times my breath-ing appeared to stop completely. Occasionally my heart beat so fiercely and loudly that a heart-attack seemed imminent. Often my whole existence was in my navel and the space between it and the small of my back. At other times I had no legs, yet I walked. Sometimes my head and hands appeared in grotesque huge forms.

Several times in meditation, for no apparent reason, I was aware that I was crying, but there were no tears.

Another time in sitting meditation, a patch of scar tissue on my right leg, the result of several operations, became alive with sensation and prickly heat causing agonizing pain. It seemed that all the blood in my body rushed into this wounded area. Nothing existed except that scar. The prickling, throbbing pain became almost unbearable. I began to sweat. I felt nauseous; I was going to be sick. I struggled to concentrate on rising and falling and 'paining, paining, paining'. It was a wretched experience; a crisis.

I clung to the rising and falling. The nauseous feeling diminished, but the scar tissue remained a violent conductor of heat and a reservoir of thousands of vibrating particles, but the pain eventually became bearable.

Eventually a blue-greenness sluggishly appeared which absorbed most of the remaining pain; the crisis had passed.

Arising simultaneously with the relief were downy fluffs of mists edged in pink. The edges became corners of solid pink that swirled into circles and prisms of infinitesimal depths and angles. There was no end to the uplifting sense of calmness that the colours created. And I returned to the rising and falling of my diaphragm.

At some point, in horror and wonder, I was aware that *I* had merged with the soothing, enticing colours. I was lost in them. Or was I beyond them? There was no 'me'! My breathing was so very slight that it almost didn't exist. Gently, forcefully, I brought 'me' out of the vastness by the only means I knew – by being mindful of my breathing. At first there was a tendency to want to remain out there – in the beyond. Gradually my breathing became more normal and I, eventually, came back to knowing that I was sitting on the floor.

I do not know if it was due to fear or to physical exertion, but after this experience I was extremely tired. I could barely move; I could not stand up. I crawled to my bed which was only a foot or two from where I was sitting. I rested, but in a strange way. It seemed important to continue my breathing, to be aware of my navel, to know that I was on the bed and not somewhere else. For a long time, I remained on the bed, being keenly aware of breath and navel – to the exclusion of all else.

That night I reported my disappearance into a world without form, time, or pain to the Acharn. He listened intently and seemed concerned. He questioned me specifically on the details of my exit before contemplating advice. 'When you become lost – when there is no one walking, nor no one sitting – then you must concentrate on *knowing*.' He calmly repeated this advice several times.

I thought that I understood. If one were able to concentrate at least one mind, on knowing, then there would be an energy to bring the other awareness back. I wondered if that was what had happened to me – one mind, or whatever it was, remained behind and it, then, startled me by making me aware that there was no thinking, no seeing, no knowing taking place.

Later, back in my room, I wondered what would have happened had I remained lost beyond the colours; if I had not been able to bring myself back to *knowing*! Did it matter that 'I' did not exist in the traditional way of thinking of 'I' and reality? It had not been painful to be there – in the beyond. Maybe that was the way of death.

That night, by the light of a single candle, I wrote:

Is existence, then, merely a thought? Was this death? It seems as I think about my experience that, indeed, I had died. I had ceased to exist. There was no 'I'; there was only a feeling of merging with the beyond, into sometime universal, a place that I seemed to know. It was soft, tranquil, floating, with no struggle. Yes, I had died and it was good – until in one horrifying moment, my mind grasped the knowledge that the 'I' was gone and my rational mind was terrified and I began to struggle to escape from this universal womb, as if I wanted to be born again. As I sit in the flickering shadows of candlelight, I wonder if I will be afraid to return to the beyond. I don't think so for it seems that I know deep in my being a truth– beyond the pain lies relief; beyond death lies birth.

## Chapter 9

Man struggles to find life outside himself, unaware
that the life he is seeking is within him.

Kahlil Gibran

ONE day slipped unnoticeably into another; all days became
one. The heavy, humid heat hung oppressively over the Chiang
Mai Valley. Monsoon clouds drifted threateningly over the
distant mountains, but never advanced with more than a few
raindrops as sentinels. To escape the intolerable heat in my
small cell, I often sat on the veranda and practised mindfulness.

In these torrid days prior to the Rains Retreat, Khaow Pansa,
there was a constant flow of men, women, and children into
the wat to make arrangements and preparations for the
ordination of their sons, brothers, cousins, and sometimes of
their fathers and grandfathers for a three-month period of contemplation and study. This was the most revered and religious
time in Theravada Buddhist countries. During the coming
months of monsoon rains, those in saffron would remain in the
wats. Except for morning alming, travelling about the countryside, so common among monks, is forbidden during the Rains
Retreat except by special permission.

For those living within our wat compound there was much
work to be done in preparing the grounds, cleaning the buildings, and generally sprucing-up the compound. Novices were
organized by the Abbot and the senior mae-chee into small
work platoons. Like clusters of orange baby ducks, these young
boys, fluttering about in their saffron robes, swept and cleaned
the temple sands with unwieldy rush brooms, carted away
refuse in wooden wheel-barrows, and, under the Abbot's
watchful eye, carefully cleaned the viharn, a process that included beating all the rugs in the viharn. Novices assigned to
the rug-cleaning detail wrapped their heads with their saffron
robes in desert Arabic style to protect themselves from the
billowing clouds of dirt and dust.

Several mae-chee organized a few novices to trim or remove

overgrown plants and flowers that grew abundantly along the compound walls and the small fence in front of the women's quarters.

During these days, I was aware of a happiness within the wat. No one said how happy they were; it was a feeling, a vibration, that flowed through me, too. My task, however, was not preparing for Khaow Pansa, but meditating – although the Abbot told me that I could watch the preparations and festivities if I were constantly mindful.

On the night before the eve of the official astrological beginning of the Rains Retreat period, I completed some meditation and ventured outside my cell. The wat was dark except for the soft glow of candle light from the viharn and the silvery radiance from the almost full moon – which would be full on the first day of the Rains Retreat. The moon's pale light touched the glass motif of the viharn, turning it into a glittering structure that seemed ethereal – a structure from fairyland. I walked to the viharn, mindful of seeing, seeing, seeing – an effort to be conscious of the seeing of such great beauty. I entered the viharn and knelt silently in the darkness near the entrance. Huge saffron candles, glowing on either side of the giant Buddha image at the front of the viharn, flickered light on several monks and the Abbot who were decorating the altars with pieces of saffron cloth and flowers.

Suddenly the Abbot, who had been bending over a potted plant, stood up, looked around, and called out to me in Thai, 'Come here! Come here!' For a moment, I feared that women were not allowed in the viharn this night and that he was calling to so inform me. It seemed that he was calling loudly. Before I could stand up, he called again, this time waving his hand as if he were waving good-bye, which in Thai custom means to come. When I reached the Abbot, he held up a long piece of saffron cloth and with just a touch of a smile, he calmly announced. 'You put this cloth around our bodhi tree. Men make things not pretty; women make them pretty.' And with that he demonstrated how he thought the cloth should be draped around the pot and then dropped the cloth to the ground for me to pick up since I could not take anything from him directly.

He stood back and watched me struggle with the cloth which was obviously too small for the job. After tying it into place with odd pieces of string that some novices produced, the little bodhi tree was, at last, decorated and ready for its trip the next day to Mount Suthep, where the people of the wat would make a pilgrimage to plant it as part of their religious activities. As I stood back to evaluate my work, the Abbot walked to my side and commented, 'It is good now; it is pretty.'

I left the candle glowing viharn to go outside and sit on the steps. As I sat there trying to be mindful of the night's special beauty, I suddenly wondered if the Abbot had consciously used the excuse of needing help in decorating the bodhi tree, the sacred tree of Buddhism, to involve me in the preparations for the Rains Retreat?

Each day now low monsoon clouds rolled and tumbled over the countryside in grey billows resembling coastal fogs capable of ubiquitous penetration. As the skies darkened and lowered, wooden shutters were closed to keep out the accompanying torrential rains, and, as one old Thai lady in the South had told me, to keep out the phii who travel in clouds and fog.

These rainy days were filled with meditation. I meditated in sitting position, walking position, and reclining. Mindfully, I ate, perspired, and swept my room. Occasionally I talked with the hunch-backed woman who several times each day pressed her face against my screen to check on me. One morning she asked me if I liked ovaltine, and in a few minutes returned with a steaming cup. She told me that she always kept a thermos of hot water and she had lots of ovaltine if I wanted more.

My stay at Wat Muang Mang began to draw to a close. When the Abbot told me that I would eventually have to leave room number four, since my cell was needed for a Thai woman who had spoken for it many months before, he assured me that he would find another place for me to stay. After careful consideration, I not only felt that it would be better if I were slowly to leave intensive meditation, but felt an internal rhythm that told me it was time to leave. Consequently, I arranged to stay for several more weeks with long-time friends in Chiang Mai so that I could still meditate most of the day and report to the meditating monks each evening.

Adjusting to the 'world' was not easy. I was fortunate that my friends were most understanding and gave me the quietest, coolest, and biggest room in their home where I could meditate as much as I chose. They understood my problems and the pain that I encountered in talking for more than a few minutes at a time. They had been careful not to ask me to eat rice, to hurry, or to talk. They had tried not to talk loudly themselves and to hush any normally loud noises.

But the extreme difficulties of adjusting to the 'world' during the first days were gone when I stood outside the gate of Wat Muang Mang, waiting for the Abbot. He had invited me to accompany him on his morning alming on this my last day in Chiang Mai. How differently I now felt as I looked through the gates into the wat compound. Only weeks ago, I had entered this gate with great trepidation, fearing where vipassana might take me. Now, as I waited in the chilly dampness of the monsoon season's pre-dawn, I understood that I had but taken the first steps into a new world. I was amazed that I had found the strength inside me to reach such depths in myself. It had not been easy, yet I knew what had happened to me could happen to anyone who made the effort.

As light came, the alming monks, one by one, silently filed through the gate as they have done for centuries. Finally I saw the Abbot coming. His robes were wrapped high around his shoulders so that only his feet, ankles, and head showed. Like a dancer projected in slow motion, he seemed to float toward me and through the gates, neither looking at me nor speaking. This floating walk of monks – the result of special steps that all monks are instructed to use, with each foot mindfully placed directly ahead of the other – was beautiful.

He turned into a lane and I followed several yards behind him. His bare feet made no sound as he padded along the wet, dirt paths, yet the faithful seemed to know when he would be arriving. As he approached house gates, men, women and children, and sometimes entire families, would emerge with food, flowers and incense for the revered man in saffron.

As I followed this gentle man on his alming rounds, I remembered that he, the son of a peasant family, had been in the saffron robes since he was twelve. Later in life, he had studied meditation in Burma for several years. Basically his entire life was his meditation, this small wat which lay outside the ancient walls of Chiang Mai, and the people who came to this simple wat to learn of the teachings of Buddha and to ask his advice on their problems.

As we wandered slowly through the narrowest of foot paths, the sun slit the heavy cloud-cover in the East to touch the ubiquitous wetness, turning the dull grey into shimmering sparkles. Simultaneously the sun's warmth seemed to release flower scents which perfumed the dewy decorated lanes with scents equalling the sun's artistry.

As I followed in the footsteps of my teacher, I reflected on the difficulties that I had encountered when I first had left intensive meditation. I had seemed weak, all my movements were snail-slow, and voices seemed too loud. The world was filled with frivolous and mundane activities, gestures and words. I had not responded with annoyance nor disdain, but with a keen desire to return to the peacefulness of the wat and the serenity of meditation.

I also remembered the Abbot's sage response when, some weeks ago, I had told him that I was experiencing a desire to stay in the wat in the peace and quiet that I had come to know. 'Some people must be monks and meditation teachers, but most people must return to their homes to care for their children and parents, to live what they've learned during vipassana, to demonstrate in living the teachings of Buddha.' I was now beginning to understand the Abbot's advice.

The Abbot completed his alming rounds and as I followed him back to the wat, I became aware of a subtle feeling of euphoria. Suddenly I realized how fortunate I had been to have had the opportunity to study Buddhism and meditation in the classical sense in a traditional setting with this warm, sensitive man.

As we entered the gate, he turned to me and invited me to share his morning meal. My interpreter joined us and together we went to the common eating hall which was occasionally used by monks and novices. Over the alms given by the faithful of Wat Muang Mang, we gathered together for these our last minutes together. I was very aware that in a few hours I would be boarding a plane that would eventually take me back to the United States. I was touched by this final gathering, but I felt that I was alone in this feeling. Perhaps others were reassured that they might see me again in another life, but whatever the reasoning it is not in the Buddhist tradition to treasure longing desires. Trying to avoid nostalgic feelings, I turned my thinking to being mindful of the present, to think of the Abbot, the young monks, novices, and temple boys who were joining us, and to think of the poignancy of the moment – that I, a foreign woman, was sitting on the floor surrounded by those in saffron robes to share a communal meal offered by others who made merit by giving food so that some people could study Buddhism and practise meditation.

Since my interpreter and I were women, we sat off to the side, but in the same room. When everyone was seated on the floor around small tables, those in saffron sang a brief Pali chant; then everyone began eating mindfully in silence, which was the custom. From an adjoining kitchen, the mae-chee from room number two served us the same hot rice gruel that I had eaten each morning during my stay in the wat.

The monks and novices ate food directly from their alms bowls while temple boys were given alms that were prepared in the wat's kitchen by several mae-chee. The Abbot's table was laden with the fruits of his morning alming and special gifts of flowers, oranges, bananas, eggs, condensed milk, rice and curries that the faithful had brought to the wat for him.

As we two women ate and occasionally whispered, I noticed the Abbot watching us. Something prompted him to send over, by a mae-chee intermediary, two oranges and two hard-boiled eggs. I was not only hungry this morning, but I was trying to gain part of the twelve pounds that I had lost during intensive meditation. I do not know whether the Abbot sensed this or not, but soon he sent over another gift – a tall glass of condensed milk for me. I struggled to drink this thick, sweet milk which the Thais consider a treat, but it was impossible. Finally I convinced my companion that she should drink it.

Spontaneously the meal ended with another Pali chant. My interpreter, dressed in white for hospital work, bade me a warm farewell, reminding me in her parting words to be mindful. The Abbot remained seated until she departed. When I looked toward him he nodded his head ever so slightly in my direction, then stood up to leave. I responded by dropping to my knees to wai in deep respect to him – my teacher.

Suddenly I was alone. The Abbot was gone; the others in saffron were filing out of the dining hall. I walked slowly across the wat compound and stopped at the gate to look back. The wat was empty except for the hunch-backed lady who was leaning over to spit out some betel-nut juice, one novice who was laundering his saffron robes at the well, and the dozen temple dogs lying in the sun on the viharn steps.

Later that day while packing at my friend's house, I found

myself wondering why I was resisting my departure from the wat and meditation. There had been frustrations, fears, discomforts, but I had experienced a fragile and soft harmony of body and mind that had culminated in an awareness of and control over both. I did not want to lose any of this.

This tranquil feeling that continued after I had left intensive meditation was due, in part, to my recent ability to be aware of the present for extended periods of time – which resulted in my being able to be mindful of the mundane tasks of living.

Over the past months, my struggles to understand mindfulness had been a constant harassment. I had continued to imagine that suddenly one day I would capture the realization of the concept of mindfulness which I conceived to be of some intellectual magnitude, but I did not and it was not. Knowing mindfulness was subtle, uncomplicated, and profoundly significant.

I discovered that one aspect of being mindful of the present was *seeing* and *knowing* mundane things. One such discovery was *seeing* an orange for the first time. I saw the saffron brilliance of an orange slice held together with the most delicate of fuzzy gossamer threads with three wet quaking bubbles of translucent juice. Mindfulness transformed this ungeometric slice of fruit which I held in my fingers into a creation of profound art that existed to the exclusion of all else.

*Knowing* the mundane tasks of eating, for example, led to a discovery of another kind of awareness. Eating became a chewing, grinding, moving – a slow-motion movement that is not just eating but a process that is minute, systematic, and controlled. How different eating in an aware fashion is from eating while talking, reading, or day-dreaming – the way that I had been accustomed to eating. By being aware of the eating process, I find it is no longer an unconscious act that exists almost outside of knowing. It becomes a mindful act that carries with it an enlightened understanding of actions. I repeatedly thought that meditation would be a boon for dieters, for the awareness of the eating process seems to eliminate the focus on food itself and places the mind's attention on the functions of the person eating it.

In a few days, I would be returning to my husband in Connecticut. How would I be able to explain to him that some of the great mysteries of the discipline of meditation were seemingly so simple and mundane. Yet, I knew that they were not simple for I had struggled for months to understand, to know, to see, to feel these nuances of being aware – of being mindful.

I finished packing, meditated, and then went for a mindful walk in my friends' garden. The sun, now momentarily free from monsoon clouds, rested languidly at the top of Mount Suthep. I stopped to watch. As I stood facing the slow descent of this tropic sun that soon I would no longer see, I became aware of witnessing this sunset in a most dramatic and unusual way.

As I watched, it was no longer a beautiful sunset that I wanted to cling to, to adore, to hold; it was more than that. The sunset was flowing through me. I seemed to possess an absorbent quality. The sunset was touching me, moving through me. I was no longer resisting nor longing for its beauty. The sunset was light, wind, movement, and space. I was seeing it *without attachment.*

My mind was still and tranquil as I stood immobile beneath the last lingering rays of sunlight, allowing them to exist without my interference. For one fleeting moment, I understood how one could at once be aware of the present and be detached.

Later that evening I wrote in my notebook.

This evening I saw my first sunset. I saw it without admiring it, loving it, or hoping that its beauty would last forever. Tonight's sunset existed without me. For a moment, I existed in a world without subject and object; I saw without attachment.

Is this the detachment that my teachers have been stressing? Is this what is meant by the ability to demonstrate loving kindness and compassion without emotion – without attachment? Is this the detachment that is the exulted goal of Buddhists?

How difficult it must be to maintain any semblance of detachment in a world of anxieties, frustrations, cruelties, sicknesses, and wars.

Connecticut is so far from here – far from this quiet country of wats, monks, and meditation. Will I be able to know a Connecticut sunset as I have known this one tonight?

## Chapter Ten

> Following others and succeeding in bookish learning
> will leave you in chains. It is far better to forget
> the big questions and to go to some quiet place to
> meditate. But that takes work!
> *The Matter of Zen* by Paul Wienpahl

OVER a year has passed since I left the land of saffron robes, glittering temples, and tropical sunsets. I have continued meditating and keeping a diary. My apprehensions about losing what I had mastered in meditation were unfounded. I was able to bring back not only the ability to meditate, but the ability to know peace and tranquillity through meditation. There have been times when I felt the need to meditate every day, times when I sought further instruction, times when a harmony existed between mind and body that seemed to make meditation unnecessary, at least for the moment.

During these past months, I have witnessed Connecticut sunrises, sunsets, and other natural phenomena in the flowing nature of awareness; I have journeyed to places reminiscent of Coleridge's fantastic 'caverns measureless to man', and to 'a sunny pleasure dome with caves of ice'; I have visited places and spaces where no form, nor colour, nor shape existed to impose upon me the need for multifarious thinking. I continue to have a better understanding and awareness of my physical and mental actions that allows me to exist without a constant battling against the forces of people, pressures, and misfortunes. My mind has a softer quality that allows things to flow through me – much like the tropical sunset flowed through me on my last night in Chiang Mai. As a result, my thinking seems more easy and more capable of handling complicated reasoning.

There have been troublesome times also in these past months. There have been times when my mind seemed as restless as it was during the first days at Wat Bovornives. But like everything else, these times and frustrations arose and faded away.

There have been times when the grosser cruelties of men and governments have caused me anguish – and more. During these times, I became aware of the tightening of muscles, increased body heat, and a faster flow of blood which thrust me into a configuration of combatancy – and I became divided into many parts. The harmony of body and mind is distracted and that, I've come to understand, is suffering. All men in all societies suffer personal anxieties and disgusts – a seemingly unfortunate outgrowth of social living.

In my case, I find that these anguishes diffuse my thoughts, my feelings, my wholeness which meditation and mindfulness can bring together again.

One day as I prepared to write in my diary, I first looked over past entries, and to my surprise I found that many entries contained the questionings of acquaintances who, for a number of reasons, are intrigued, puzzled, and sceptical about meditation and its potential value. The same questions seem to appear again and again.

'How can I meditate? I can't possibly go to Asia and study with Buddhist monks. I don't have the time, nor place, nor a teacher. I don't understand what value this kind of meditation has in a highly technological and fast moving society where

emphasis is on achieving and being successful. Why should I deny my ego and become a "nothing"? I have to earn a living, I can't sit around contemplating my navel! Looking inside oneself seems an irrational and subjective exercise.'

To those who ask such questions (as I honestly must say I once also asked), I respond that Theravada Buddhist meditation is not a physical journey, but an internal exploration that can take place in a prison cell, an office, a space capsule, on another planet, even in one's home as remote from Asia as the rolling hills of Connecticut.

When I returned to my home in Connecticut, I organized an alcove in my living room where I could meditate. Each afternoon between four o'clock and five, I sat in this alcove before a red, saffron, and emerald green sand and tempera painting of the Buddhist wheel of life, and a few sticks of jasmine-scented incense.

Preparation for meditation seems important. I often take a shower before meditation or read some passages from a book on Buddhism or merely a book on Asian history. During meditation, I often become very aware of tight-fitting clothing, so I often sit nude or with a bathrobe around my shoulders.

I have long abandoned the need to know how long meditation lasts, but I estimate that my meditation varies from fifteen minutes to an hour, sometimes even longer. There are times when I easily go into meditation, but there are other times when I struggle to concentrate my mind on the awareness of my breathing. I never force meditation nor try to sit for a specific period of time. I become part of the experience, gently bringing my jumping mind back to my breath, and try not to become disturbed if meditation reverts to undisciplined stages similar to the struggling episodes that I encountered in the initial days at Wat Bovornives. Like all other things, this rampant obsession of the mind to defy stilling will also pass. Often, after what I might consider an unsatisfactory experience, I find that the next day my meditation may be deep, smooth, and quite refreshing.

It now seems unimportant to have a specific place to meditate. Recently, I've found myself drawn to meditate in various parts of my home. At the moment, there is a place in my bedroom that is most attractive to my internal sense, so I meditate there, abandoning the idea that one must have a 'place' in order to meditate.

This urge to meditate, to be refurbished, to become tranquil can occur at any time or place. One night last autumn I was strangely drawn to the beauty of a moonlit night; there was a strong urge to become part of the night and its beauty. After finishing my kitchen work, I went outside for a walk in the woods with my little puppy. The powerful beauty of the night stirred my soul. The large silvery moon cast an eerie glow on my world, darkly engraving towering spruce trees against the lighter spaces between earth and its heavens. As the puppy trotted obediently and silently beside me, our shadowy figures against the ground were as daguerreotypes of days past. Almost without provocation, except by the incredibly soft beauty of the night, I felt the desire to meditate. I sat down on a grassy spot and my puppy sat by my side.

For awhile I sat silently to enjoy the multitude of delicate hues and geometries created by the touching of the moon on the woods, rocks, and grasses.

Entrance into meditation was easy and natural, taking me into a quietness of no-thinking and timelessness. When meditation was finished, I slowly opened my eyes to find my little dog sitting directly in front of me, watching me with ears erect. The moon, no longer among the spruce trees, had moved into larger spaces diminishing the contrasting blackness of the ethereal forest and the heavens. I found that I was covered with a heavy layer of shimmering dew. I don't know how long I had been meditating, but it was unimportant. I remained sitting on the dewy grass as a flow of nature swept through me. The moon, the shadows, the dew, my dog, and I were one in the silence of the moonlight night. I was aware of the omniscient feeling of detachment, a detachment from knowing the world through myself. I was one with the flow of the universe. I was not separate. I had now known a moonrise as I had known my first sunset in the hills of northern Thailand.

Having a routine for meditation is certainly desirable, but one must be prepared to follow an internal need, or rhythm to meditate, for it seems that the natural calls to meditate can produce the most extraordinary experiences.

During this past year, there were times when I experienced a consuming desire to be with a meditation teacher. Six months after I had returned from intensive meditation in Thailand, I felt this need very strongly. I had supposed that in the West, teachers of the Theravada tradition would be non-existent. But to my surprise, after minimum inquiry, I learned of a ten-day meditation retreat being conducted in the Baltimore-Washington area and I attended. At this retreat, held at a remote church retreat facility, a Thai, a former monk, conducted the session which required total silence, at least six hours of group meditation per day, and an equal number of hours of individual meditation. In this environment, with no commitments but to meditate, I found the opportunity to return to the state of oneness and tranquillity that I had experienced in intensive meditation at Wat Muang Mang. It was a refurbishing of the well-spring, a returning to the essence of oneness, a rejuvenating which I was able to bring back to my work-a-day world. My state of heightened awareness did lessen in time when I returned to the distractions of my life, but this state need not disappear fast. I decided that after this intensive meditation session, I would practise meditation more often in order to maintain this state of awareness. I did and I was moderately successful at my attempt.

We, in the West, worry too much about having a 'guru' before we can start meditation. I have come to think that there is much merit in a popular saying among advanced meditators: 'A teacher is there when the student is ready'.

Surprisingly, I am finding that more and more meditation centres and teachers are available in the West. One should not be discouraged from beginning meditation with the excuse that there are no teachers – for there are. While I believe that it is risky and probably impossible for an average person to begin *intensive* meditation without an instructor,

I also believe that one can begin learning to concentrate the mind alone by merely watching one's breath. There is much to be done before one is ready to begin intensive meditation such as I experienced in Asia.

For those who ask me how to begin to meditate, I say first that your attitude is most important. You must be willing to persevere every day with gentle persistence and to understand that true meditation takes a long time to develop. There is nothing esoteric about getting into meditation. It is like learning to read. First one must learn the alphabet. Learning to concentrate the mind is the first step before one can go deeper and deeper into meditation. Learning to concentrate the mind is one of the most difficult tasks that a human being is ever asked to undertake. To understand how difficult it is, I ask you to do the following (at this very moment); close your eyes and begin breathing in and out ten times, then fix your attention on each breath as it comes in and then as it is released. Count each breath if you like. 'One – in; one – out. Two – in; two – out' or say 'breathing – in' – 'breathing – out'.

How many times did your mind jump to fix itself on something other than the breath coming in and going out? Based on my own experiences, it undoubtedly touched on a dozen thoughts, all of a very varied nature. This is the beginning stage of learning to concentrate and this can be practised and practised until the count of ten breaths in and out can be accomplished without excessive diversions. There is nothing exotic about watching one's breath, it is after all the life force, and there is nothing unusual about not being able to do it in the initial stages of work.

The idea of MUST throws most people off. Some schools of meditation programme their students to meditate twenty minutes, twice a day. During the beginning stages, this amount of time may seem excessive and result in a feeling that one cannot do it. Twenty minutes of concentration, at first, may seem an impossible task and many people are put off by the *must* aspect and eventually give up. I believe that if one tries serious meditation five to ten minutes a day in the initial stages, that is sufficient. But don't fool yourself. It takes time. As one's concentration becomes more acute, the time spent in meditation will expand by itself. In time you will pleasantly discover that meditation is not only a natural mental function, but is, as well, a positive centering process.

There is no definite position that one should assume in meditation, but one must be comfortable. You can sit on a straight-backed chair, or tuck your legs in a lotus position or half-lotus, or sit in the Japanese fashion – on your knees with a pillow between your buttocks and your heels. You must have firm support with your back firm so that the curve of the back is natural with no slump. Distend your 'tummy'. Be aware of your breath touching your nostrils, or you can focus on the rising and falling of your diaphragm. Tilt your head slightly downward, eyes not quite straight ahead, and eyelids closed. Nothing should be touching your 'tummy' or restricting any part of your body. Wear a loose-fitting garment or nothing if the temperature is appropriate. Make certain that the body is in a comfortable position. After you are comfortable with your back in a firm position, begin watching the breath. Don't become discouraged. Be mindful of your wandering mind and gently bring it back to watching the breath. Meditation is not letting your mind wander into daydreaming; it is just the opposite – a discipline. One goal in meditation is to learn to control the mind to develop one-pointedness of the mind.

Being mindful can be done while walking, riding the train to work, doing routine work like raking leaves, pulling weeds, washing dishes, scrubbing floors. One can watch the breath at any time, thus keeping the ability to concentrate by constantly training the mind.

In our daily lives, being mindful can be useful to counter such feelings as jealousy, anger, and fear. One day I was able to conquer fear by employing mindfulness. Although a pilot with some experience, I occasionally find myself being overcome with fear while flying. One day soon after I had left the Washington, D.C., intensive meditation session, I was in the front seat of a single-engine plane with my husband, an experienced pilot with an instrument rating and lots of flying experience, who was piloting. As we neared the greater metropolitan area of New York City we flew into a rain storm. Our airplane radios screeched with static and with the garbled voices of seemingly hundreds of pilots trying to communicate with control towers.

Our light plane, buffeted by strong storm winds, repeatedly bucked and bounced, dropping and soaring upward with alarming swiftness. Visibility was zero; rain pounded on the wind shield. I was becoming more and more uncomfortable with the flying conditions, then like lightning, fear struck me. I seemed unable to control it. My hands were wet with cold perspiration; my heart thumped in my chest, my stomach, my throat; my muscles tightened throughout my body. I wanted out of the plane. For several moments this fear held me captive. Then, for some reason that I can't account for, I decided to be mindful of my breathing in an attempt to still my mind. I began breathing in and breathing out; breathing in and breathing out. At first my breathing was jerky and fast, then as I fastened to my breathing, my breath became more regular and softer. I then focused my attention to the fear which was affecting various parts of my body. As I became aware of and examined the gnawing sensations in my stomach, they slowly . . . very slowly . . . ebbed. Then I focused on another part of my body caught up in this fear. As I examined the spot, the muscles relaxed and the cramping fear disintegrated. Soon this fear which only minutes before had consumed my mental state was gone; I had liberated myself from fear . . . which after all was only a mental condition that I had created within myself. Soon I was able to return to being helpful to my husband.

The Buddha is reported to have said to beginning meditators: 'Begin and continue' – and that is my advice also. Too often we spend our time reading about meditation and never get around to trying it.

Theravada Buddhist meditation is a *teachable discipline* that can help us focus on our own nature. Meditation is not in any way becoming a 'nothing', as understood in the Western sense of the word, but a becoming that involves greater understanding of our own being, which makes us more aware, more perceptive to our environment and to those around us.

Meditation, it seems to me, is among many things a learning to still the mind, to control it, to centre the mind's potential energy. In this quietness or condensation of the mind's energy, the mind expands and is capable of producing more acute realizations. Consequently, and in time, the body and mind seem to come together in a harmony or a centering because separateness, or duality, of the body and mind is diminished and at times even absent. It seems, in essence, that it is this separateness of body and mind which prevents humans from knowing their true selves and is consequently the source of much struggle, of much unhappiness, of much suffering.

The process of meditation seems to involve a shedding of desires, of the need for unnecessary possessions, of a demanding ego, of the importance of the trite, superfluous, loud or ostentatious. When these fall away – as they will in meditation – it becomes possible to know something of the true self. In this new state minus all these hindering distracting trappings, the mind can be centred and achieve personal equanimity.

To those who struggle to reconcile Christianity and Buddhism, I say that it is not important to find similarities and differences, to search for holes in logic, nor to take a missionary stand for either. Buddhist thinking is predicated on beliefs dramatically different from those predominant in other cultures. Western cultures, for example, emphasize dualism in man and nature, between the world and God, between the physical and the mental.

Focus in Buddhism is on the individual. Perhaps this could be better understood by considering that there exists a force in the universe – and in us – which can become diffused and disorganized. Meditation is a technique to restore the unity of this potential in us.

To understand Buddhism and meditation it is important not to distrust, not to dissect, not to be cynical, and above all not to encounter Buddhist thought with a 'hard' mind. The Thais say that to understand, one must possess a 'soft' mind so that things can flow through it unhindered. It is often preconceived frames of reference and windows of logic that prevent us of the West from comprehending.

When I try to answer well-meaning people's questions about Buddhism, and particularly about meditation, I find that my answers are often unfulfilling – often for one very obvious reason. *Understanding meditation is experiential.*

To those who say that they must read more before they can understand meditation, and to those who say that such experiences as I personally have had in meditation are truly unbelievable, I answer only that there is a calmness, an understanding, a harmony in my life which has developed as a result of meditation. And I say to you who question, as the wise old Abbot at Wat Bovornives said to me so many times: 'One's Self Is the Big Book'.

## Meditation Practice

Where tireless striving stretches its arms toward
perfection
Where the mind is led forward by . . . ever widening
thoughts
Into that heaven of freedom let me awake . . .
                                        Rabindranath Tagore

INHERENT in Theravada Buddhist meditation is self-analysis –
a willingness to examine oneself. The Buddhist concept of
being *Awake* is the realization that all of us can save ourselves
from our own suffering. All of us have within us the potential
to win our own freedom.

The essence of Buddhism is a study of the 'four noble truths'
as before mentioned: that unhappiness or suffering exists in
our lives, that there is a cause for this suffering (such as
clinging to life, to people, to things), that there is a way out
of this unhappiness. The way out, according to the Buddhists,
is to follow a rational path that will change or perfect thought,
word, and deed. This way out is known as the 'eight-fold
path' of 1) right understanding – coming to know that all is
not right, to identify what is wrong, and replace ignorance
with knowledge and insight; 2) right resolve or motives – the
honest decision to do something to improve oneself; 3) right
speech – elimination of idle chatter, gossip, backbiting, harsh
speech, lying. To talk as if one wanted to change for the
better; 4) right action – acting with honesty, love, humility;
5) right means of livelihood – pursuing a job that will help
one develop one's own positive potentials as well as understand better those around us; 6) right effort – the development
of insight and will power – a will power to change; 7) right
mindfulness – learning to be constantly and acutely aware of

the nature of all thoughts, words, and actions; 8) right meditation or concentration. According to the Venerable Dr Saddhatissa, 'Meditation and its counterpart in daily life – mindfulness (sati) – form together the essence of the Buddha's teaching,' and the last phase of the path leading to the cessation of unhappiness or suffering.

ONE IS NEVER TOO OLD TO BEGIN NOR TOO YOUNG
TO LEARN MEDITATION

So, let's begin.

There are many meditation practices. Here is one of the most widely taught, 'Anapanasati' or Mindfulness of Breathing. This method comes to us directly from the time of the Buddha.

*MENTAL ATTITUDE:*

When you possess greed, anger, and delusion, it will be difficult to find freedom and peace. Love, goodness, and humility must be cultivated. Meditation is actually the training of one's own mind – and heart.

Mental attitude is most important. Be open. Have a 'soft' or open mind. Be willing to try. Let go.

*TIME AND PLACE:*

Don't put off meditation, if you really want it! In the initial days don't deceive yourself by saying, 'I have no time'. Be firm. Find time. There is always *some* time.

Look for it. Early morning, in the evening, during lunch hour, to and from work, perhaps before the evening meal. It is, of course, desirable to have a quiet, relaxing atmosphere for meditation.

*POSITION:*

You must be COMFORTABLE. You can sit on a straight-backed chair, or tuck your legs in a lotus or half-lotus position, tailor fashion, or sit in Japanese style on your knees with a pillow between your buttocks and your heels. If sitting on a chair, keep your feet flat on the floor, legs uncrossed. Back up-right. Neck held up. Eyelids closed. Hands clasped loosely in lap. Relax. Do not struggle. Just let go.

*Mindfulness of Breathing:*

So simple – when you know how. Focus attention on nostrils. Become acutely aware of the breath as it enters your nostrils. Watch it carefully. Follow the breath. Follow it into the nostrils and then as it comes out. Continue to watch the breath – coming in and going out – coming in and going out. Keep the mind on the breath. Try to keep the mind on the breath inside the body – inside the emptiness of the body.

Your mind may flit away. Bring the mind *gently* back. Then continue watching the breath. Do not struggle. Do not try too hard. *Don't become discouraged.* Be patient with yourself. Be good to yourself. This is no conflict. Let quietness prevail. Peace . . . peace . . . peace. Just let go. Let peacefulness softly wipe away the impatience, the anxiety, the frustrations. Feel. Begin to feel a blissful inner peace. Enjoy this new experience. Quiet . . . beautiful. Continue breathing until it is smooth-flowing, regular and soft.

Now direct the mind to one spot – I suggest a spot on the upper lip. Focus here firmly. Your breath will become very gentle and slow – almost indiscernible. Don't worry. Nothing will happen to you. Stay with it. Feel the flow. Let go. Let it all drift away. Let go. Let go. Nothing else matters now.

Feel freedom from fear, anger, greed. Feel them disappearing. Continue breathing in and breathing out. Breathing in and breathing out. Breathing in and breathing out.

The above instructions have been prepared so that, if you like, you can read them very, very slowly and with long pauses between the various sections onto a tape recorder and then in your initial days of learning mindfulness of breathing, you can play the tape to yourself.

The advanced stage of this meditation is called insight or vipassana meditation – where mind (and heart) is still and knowledge and wisdom are awakened – where knowledge of one's self and one's potential is developed.

After you are able to still your mind for a period of time without intensive struggling, you might want to seek out a teacher to guide you in more rigorous steps of meditation. Meditation centres and teachers are becoming more and more available in the West – in England, Germany, Australia, New Zealand, Canada, the United States, and other countries.

## Suggested Reading

King, Winston: *A Thousand Lives Away*, Alec R. Allenson Inc., New York, 1965

Ross, Nancy Wilson: *Three Ways of Asian Wisdom*, Simon and Schuster, New York, 1966

Saddhatissa, H.: *The Buddha's Way*, George Braziller Inc., New York, 1972

Suzuki, Shunryu: *Zen Mind, Beginner's Mind*, Weatherhill, New York and Tokyo, 1970

Swearer, Donald (ed.): *Secrets of the Lotus*, Collier-Macmillan, New York and London, 1971

# Glossary

MANY of the words in this text are translations from Pali, Sanskrit, and Thai. The sounds of these words are difficult to duplicate since there are sounds in those languages for which there are no English equivalents. The usual phonetic system therefore seems inappropriate. I have consequently devised for use in this glossary a system to approximate the sounds of these words.

Abhidhamma (ah-bee-dtam-mah), the philosophical interpretations of the Buddhist doctrines

acharn (ah-jarn), teacher or master

anatta (ah-nah-tah), egolessness, no-selfness, doctrine that there is no constant, unchanging self

anicca (ah-nee-jah), impermanence, not stable, change

anapanasati (ah-nah-pahn-nah-sah-tee), mindfulness of breathing, meditation reportedly practised in the time of the Buddha

Ayutthaya (ah-yuut-tah-yah), capital of Siam, or Thailand, from 1350 until 1767

bhikkhu (bee-khu), Pali word for Buddhist monk

bhikkhuni (bee-khu-nee), a female bhikkhu

Bhumipol Adulyadej (Bum-ee-pone Ah-dune-yah-det), King of Thailand since 1946

bodhi tree (bow-dee), or the bo (fig) tree called the Tree of Enlightenment or Wisdom under which Siddartha became enlightened. Both bodhi and bo are often capitalized

bodhisattva (bow-dee-sat-vah), appears especially in Mahayana Buddhist thinking. Refers to one who has attained enlightenment yet elects to remain among men to help others to reach salvation

Buddha (buu-dta), the awakened or enlightened one. Siddartha Gotama (or Gautama) of the Sakya Muni clan. Founder of Buddhism

Buddhadhamma (buu-dta-dtam-mah), the teachings or doctrines of Buddha

Buddhada (buu-dtat-tat), famous elderly monk, writer, and teacher living in Thailand

Buddhism (buu-dizm), a philosophy, religion, a code of ethics

chai-yen (chai-yen), Thai word for cool heart or to have patience

Chao Phraya (chow-pra-yah). Thai phrase meaning noble lord, also the name of the major river that flows through Thailand southward into the Gulf of Siam

Chao Tii (chow-tee), the spirit of the house or dwelling

chedi (jay-dee), edifice usually containing ashes or relics of a revered person

dhamma (dtam-mah), the teachings of Buddha, the law, the way, nature, or reality

dukka (dtuu-kah), suffering, pain, unhappiness, sorrow, misery, or simply that which is unsatisfactory

eight-fold path, the way out of unhappiness. It includes 1) 'samma ditthi' or right understanding 2) 'samma sankappa' or right resolve or motives 3) 'samma vada' or right speech 4) 'samma kammanta' or right action 5) 'samma ajiva' or right means of livelihood 6) 'samma vayama' or right effort 7) 'samma sati' or right mindfulness 8) 'samma samadhi' or right meditation or concentration

farang (far-rahng), Caucasian foreigner

four noble truths, the Buddha's teachings of 1) 'dukka' or suffering 2) 'tanha' or clinging 3) 'nirodha' or the concept that there is a way out 4) 'magga', the path or the way out – or in other words 1) that there is suffering and unhappiness in life 2) that this unhappiness comes from our greed, our desires, our self-centredness 3) that this excessive egocentrism can be eliminated and 4) that this can be achieved by following the eight fold path

Gautama (gow-tah-mah), sometimes spelled Gotama. Siddartha Gautama is said to have been born in 543 BC on the day of a full moon in what is present-day Nepal in Lumbini Garden. He became known as the Buddha

guti (guu-tee), abode of a monk

guru (guu-ruu), spiritual guide

Hinduism (hin-duu-izm), religious philosophies of the Hindus

Jataka Tales (jah-tah-kah), tales emanating from India of the lives of the Buddha

kamma (kah-mah), Pali word. A law of cause and effect

karma (kar-mah). Sanskrit word. Same meaning as kamma

karuna (gha-ruu-nah), compassion

Khaow Pansa (cow pahn-sah), Thai word referring to the three months' residence in the wat by monks during the rainy season

klong (klong), canal

mae-chee (meh-chee), Thai word for nun

Mahanikai (mah-hah-nee-kai), largest group of Buddhist monks in Thailand

Mahayana Buddhism (mah-hah-yah-nah), one of the schools of Buddhism. Found in Tibet, Sikkim, China, Korea, Japan, Vietnam

Mekong (meh-kong), major river in Southeast Asia

metta (meh-tah), loving kindness

Middle Way, according to the Buddha, the proper path of conduct for humans to follow. A path without extremes of any kind – without excessive indulgences or excessive asceticism

mudita (muu-dee-tah), satisfaction or joy in the successes of others

nimitta (nim-ee-tah), conceptual image that can be 'seen' in meditation

Nibbana (nib-bahn-nah), ultimate realization or perfection, freedom from rebirth

Nirvana (near-vah-nah), Sanskrit form of the Pali word Nibbana

Pali (bah-lee), language used in Theravada Buddhist writings. Supposedly the language in which the Buddha spoke

panna (pahn-yah), wisdom

phii (pee), ghosts or spirits

phroom (prome), supermundane being

preta (preh-tah), hungry ghost or spirit

Rains Retreat, the three month period of rains when the monks reside within the wat. A special time to be ordained and to be a monk for those months

sala (sah-lah), open-air hall or resting place for travellers samadhi (sah-mah-dtee), tranquillity state of meditation

samsara (sahm-sah-rah), repeating cycle of becoming – birth and death

Sangha (sahng-gah), Buddhist monastic community

Sanskrit (sans-krit), ancient language of India. Religious texts of both Hinduism and Buddhism have been written in Sanskrit

sati (sah-dtee), mindfulness, awareness

satipatthana (sah-tee-pah-tah-nah), four foundations of mindfulness, a meditation practice that stresses mindfulness of body, feelings, of the mind and its changing nature and of different aspects of Buddha's teachings

satori (sah-tor-ee), sudden enlightenment found in the Zen tradition

sukka (suu-kha), happiness

tamboon (dtam-buun), to do good, to make merit

tanha (tan-hah), desire, craving, clinging; cause for rebirth

Thailand (tie-land), country in Asia formerly known as Siam

Theravada Buddhism (dtair-rah-vad-dta), literally 'The Way of the Elders'. More akin to the original teachings of Buddha. Flourishes in Burma, Cambodia, Laos, Thailand, and Sri Lanka

Thammayut (dtam-mah-yut), means 'Those Adhering to the Law'. Strictest group of Buddhist monks in Thailand

upekkah (uu-bay-kah), state of equanimity and balance

viharn (wee-harn), large temple hall where lay people meet to listen to the monks

vipassana (wee-pah-sah-nah), insight meditation

wai (like the letter 'Y'), a gesture of respect made by placing the hands together to resemble a lotus bud and then placing the hands before the face

wat (watt), the temple compound which includes several buildings including the viharn

Wat Bovornives (bah-vor-nee-wet), royal wat in Bangkok, Thailand

Wat Muang Mang (muung-mang), meditation wat near Chiang Mai, Thailand

## About The Author

**Jane Hamilton-Merritt's** life has taken her from a dairy farm in the American mid-West to East Africa as a bush pilot, through various countries of Asia as a teacher and writer – including several assignments as a war correspondent-photographer in Vietnam, Laos and Thailand – to living with opium-growing minority peoples in South East Asia.

Born in Hamilton, Indiana, she studied at Ball State University and then did graduate work at the University of the Ryukyus in Japan, the American University in Washington, and at Vanderbilt. She has a Ph D in Asian Studies from Union Graduate School, Yellow Springs, Ohio, and has taught at universities and colleges in the United States and Asia.

Her 1969 newspaper series on young soldiers from Miami County, Ohio, fighting in South East Asia was nominated for a Pulitzer Prize in International Reporting. She was the 1969 Grand Prize winner (and the first woman recipient) of the Inland Daily Press Association annual contest for front-line combat photography. Her photo-essay 'Youth of South East Asia' has travelled the U.S., and she has published two of a projected series of books for young adults on the peoples and cultures of South East Asia, *Boonmee and the Lucky White Elephant* and *Lahu Wildlife*.

## About the Artist

**Sanya Wongaram,** the Thai artist whose ink drawings illustrate *A Meditator's Diary,* was born in 1943 in Bangkok, where he received a university degree in Graphic Art (Silpakorn University) in 1969. He now teaches at Chulalongkorn University.

He has exhibited in Thailand, Italy, Spain, Denmark and at the Tenth Biennale in Sao Paulo, Brazil in 1969. He won Second Prize at the 19th National Exhibition in Bangkok in 1969, and Third Prize at the 22nd Exhibition in 1973. In the same year he was awarded a Netherlands Fellowship at the Rietveld Akademie, Amsterdam (1973-75), and a Purchase Award by the Netherlands Government.